GOD'S DIVINE
PLANS FOR MARRIAGE

KINGDOM CHOICES
MARRIAGE EDITION • BOOK I

Krista Nicole

GOD'S DIVINE
PLANS FOR MARRIAGE

A GUIDE TO UNDERSTANDING PEOPLE AS WANTS, NEEDS & DESIRES

INNATE DREAMS
PUBLISHING

Scripture quotations marked BSB are taken from The Holy Bible, Berean Study Bible, BSB Copyright ©2016, 2020 by Bible Hub. Used by Permission. All Rights Reserved Worldwide.

Scripture quotations marked NKJV are taken from the New King James Version® of the Bible. Copyright © 1982 by Thomas Nelson. Used by permission. All rights reserved.

Scripture quotations marked NIV are taken from the New International Version® of the Bible. Copyright © 1973, 1978, 1984, 2011 by Biblica Inc. ® Used by permission. All rights reserved worldwide.

Scripture quotations marked ESV are taken from the English Standard Version® of the Bible. Copyright © 2001 by esvliteralword.com ® Used by permission. All rights reserved worldwide.

Scripture quotations marked ASV are taken from the American Standard Version® of the Bible. Copyright © BibileGateway.com. Used by permission. All rights reserved.

Scripture quotations marked KJV are taken from the King James Version® of the Bible. Copyright © BibleGateway.com. Used by permission. All rights reserved.

Scripture quotations marked AKJV are taken from the Authorized (King James) Version® of the Bible ('the KJV'). Copyright © BibileGateway.com. Used by permission. All rights reserved.

Scripture quotations marked GNT are taken from the Good News Translation® (Today's English Version, Second Edition) Copyright © 1992 American Bible Society. Used by permission. All rights reserved.

Scripture quotations marked AMPC are taken from the Amplified Bible, Classic Edition® of the Bible ('the KJV'). Copyright © 2015 Registered in the United States Patent and Trademark Office by The Lockman Foundation. Used by permission. All rights reserved.

Scripture quotations marked NLT are taken from the Holy Bible, New Living Translation, copyright © 1996, 2004, 2015 by Tyndale House Foundation. Used by permission of Tyndale House Publishers, Inc., Carol Stream, Illinois 60188. All rights reserved.

Scripture quotations marked CEV are taken from the Contemporary English Version - 2nd Edition, Copyright © 2006 by American Bible Society. Used by permission. All Rights Reserved.

Boldface type in the Scripture quotations indicates the author's emphasis.

GOD'S DIVINE PLANS FOR MARRIAGE:
A Guide to Understanding People as Wants, Needs & Desires

Kingdom Choices™: Marriage Edition–Book I

GodsDivinePlansForMarriage.com

For speaking engagements and special discounts for bulk purchases, please contact:
Innate Dreams Publishing, LLC
Contact@InnateDreamsPublishing.com
www.InnateDreamsPublishing.com

ISBN 979-8-9883991-1-7 (Paperback)   ISBN 979-8-9883991-2-4 (Hardcover)
ISBN 979-8-9883991-0-0 (Ebook)   ISBN 979-8-9883991-4-8 (Audiobook)

Copyright © 2024 Krista Nicole Owens
All Rights Reserved
First Edition

All rights reserved. No part of this publication may be reproduced, distributed, or transmitted in any form or by any means, including photocopying, recording, or other electronic or mechanical methods without the prior written permission of the publisher. For permission requests, solicit the publisher via the email below.

Innate Dreams Publishing, LLC   Contact@InnateDreamsPublishing.com

Innate Dreams Publishing and colophon and Kingdom Choices (book series) and colophon are trademarks of Innate Dreams Publishing, LLC.

To

_____

From

_____

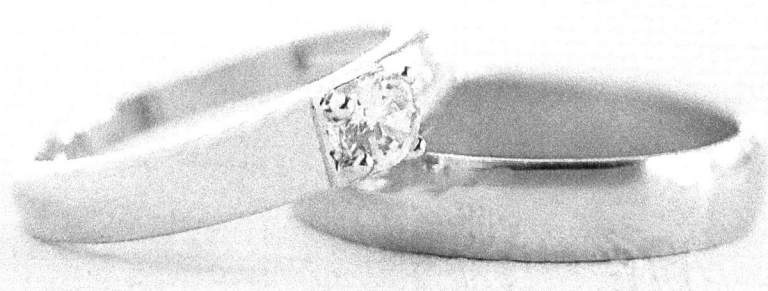

DEDICATION

This book is dedicated to my beloved, beautiful mother, Kathy Bowden, who inspired me my *entire* life to *use my brain and think*! The result of spiritual growth should *always* produce growth in the ability to *think*! Thank you, Mom, for providing life principles for a balanced life! Thank you for teaching and instilling morals and values that benefited my brothers and me, and many others, for a lifetime! And your sacrifices were not in vain! You molded and shaped me, and your reward is here! I love you and thank you! You created a legacy!

Most importantly, this book is dedicated to the Father God, the Son–Jesus, The Christ and the Holy Spirit. Thank you!

ACKNOWLEDGMENT

Special thank you to pastors Apostle Dr. Fred L. Hodge Jr. and First Lady Linda Hodge, founders of Living Praise Christian Center. Thank you for pouring, depositing, and watering seeds of wisdom for twenty-one years after I became a follower and servant for Jesus, The Christ.

Special thank you to Dr. Matthew L. Stevenson, III and Dr. Kamilah Stevenson, founders of All Nations Worship Assembly. Their ministry helped set me free beginning in 2016 from a place of bondage in my previous marriage, and I have been on a course of a newly discovered purpose ever since. Although I don't know them both personally, I have been a distant student of their teachings for seven years and counting. I am grateful for their wisdom, boldness, and obedience to Jesus, The Christ.

Special thank you to Apostle and Prophetess Kayla Reese, founder of Kayla Reese Ministries. Thank you for being a sister-in-Christ "rock" for me, pastor, spiritual covering, intercessor, apostle, teacher, and prophetess. As God uses me to heal, teach, and impart wisdom, you're always there when I need strength, wisdom, understanding, and refreshing! I love you forever.

Special thank you to all those who have imparted Godly wisdom pertaining to life, marriage, individual growth, and purpose (*both directly and indirectly*), those who took me under their wings! Thank you, Jamee Yurkovich, Patricia and Loren Duruso (for those early years of discipleship and foundational teachings), and Dijon and Rochelle Bishop (who taught me self-worth, self-love, and so much more). I love you all!

Special thank you to the ministries that created and developed a major part and impact on my life's journey…thus far. Thank you, All Nations Worship Assembly (Chicago and New York), Living Praise Christian Center, and Kayla Reese Ministries. Thank you for launching me to my next level and dimension in God.

Thank you to my amazing and exceptional children for their patience and understanding during this seven-year process. Thank you to my family and true friends for your unconditional love! Specifically, thank you to my brother, Brandon Bowden, for your consistent words of encouragement.

Thank you to every reader who receives *Godly wisdom* from this book to experience a powerful marriage. You have blessed me, both near and from afar.

NOTE FROM THE AUTHOR

This book will *forever* transform how you view potential mates based on what matters—Godly character—as well as how you examine yourself and motives! After reading (or listening) to this book, you will be prepared to choose the lifelong partner God intends for you to marry!

I received the concept of this book, *God's Divine Plans for Marriage: A Guide to Understanding People as Wants, Needs & Desires*, in January 2017, and it was birthed from a revelation from God as an intrusive thought. And more definitions, concepts, and Godly wisdom poured out in the form of chapters. I KNEW this was a SPECIAL book being written to change minds and hearts to align with Godly principles and create marriages that God **orchestrated** for several generations (and beyond) and societies where so many values and the true purpose of marriage have been lost! What I didn't know was it would take seven years to complete!

I completed the foundation (the chapters, concepts, etc.) in February 2018 and thought the book was finished. However, for the next six years, from 2018–2024, more wisdom was added from personal experiences, observations, and revelation directly from God as I embarked on my journey as a single woman after my divorce in 2017. God was writing *through me* to prepare you for your Kingdom marriage…as He was preparing me.

Seven years later, in 2024, *God's Divine Plans for Marriage* became available worldwide. The Holy Spirit wrote this book through me. This book is my epistle.

> *"Therefore, brethren, stand fast and hold the traditions which you were taught, whether by word or our epistle."*
>
> -Paul, the Apostle
>
> 2 Thessalonians 2:15

CONTENTS

DEDICATION vii

PRELUDE xiii

CHAPTER 1.
CRITICAL DECISION-MAKING AREAS OF LIFE:
MARRIAGE / SPOUSES, CAREERS, AND HOME REGIONS.. 1

CHAPTER 2.
DEFINING "WANTS" AND "NEEDS" 5

CHAPTER 3.
THE ORIGIN OF SOLID DECISION-MAKING:
THE BREAKDOWN OF PSALM 37:4 25

CHAPTER 4.
THE DEFINITION OF "DESIRES": INTRO TO
"NEEDED WANTS" A.K.A. GOD'S DESIRES 39

CHAPTER 5.
THE DANGER OF MISINTERPRETING PSALM 37:4 49

CHAPTER 6.
THE "COUNTERFEITS": UNDERSTANDING
AND IDENTIFYING A "CLOSE-FIT" 61

CHAPTER 7.
PREPARATION & PURSUIT 89

CHAPTER 8.
"FALLING IN LOVE" VERSUS "DISCOVERY OF LOVE"... 107

CHAPTER 9.
**NO ONE IS PERFECT: DON'T MISTAKE
"NEEDS" FOR "THE PERFECT MATCH"** 119

CHAPTER 10.
"TIMING AND WINDOWS" & BEING "PRIME ENOUGH". 131

CHAPTER 11.
**THE FIFTH AND SIXTH OPTION TYPES:
"NEITHERS" & "LIKES"** 145

CHAPTER 12.
**THE REVERSAL EFFECT: WHEN "DESIRES"
TURN SIMPLY INTO "WANTS" & "NEEDS"** 149

CHAPTER 13.
"MIXED-MATCHED TYPES": IT IS VERY POSSIBLE 161

CHAPTER 14.
**THE POWER OF ALL DECISIONS: RIGHT,
WRONG, PAST, PRESENT, AND FUTURE** 187

CHAPTER 15.
"SIMPLE" TRUTHS ABOUT CHOICES & OPTIONS 207

ABOUT THE AUTHOR 217

PRELUDE

Have you ever heard the saying, "Life is about choices"? Well, if you haven't, you have now! I first heard this saying in my early 20s and had no clue as to the depth of these four seemingly simple words. I remember thinking to myself… *Yes, we have to make choices in life daily…so, in essence, that is correct. Not very "deep."* Well, what I grew to understand through life experiences is our choices literally shape our lives, and our lives are a *sum* total of all the choices we've made thus far, as my former pastor of twenty-one years, would so eloquently put it.

If the choices we make, in fact, shape our lives, *choices*, in general, are *extremely* important and worth understanding. However, before we can evaluate our choices, we must first understand, in depth, the most common types of choices we make from a list of option types. We need to understand, specifically, the "root" that drives our decision-making process to a particular *option* that **becomes** a choice. I have categorized these options. The main common types of options are "*Wants*," "*Needs*," and "*Desires*." The other three are "*Counterfeits*," "*Likes*," and "*Neithers*."

This book will explain the *influence* in which our *soulical* experiences (from our mind, will, intellect, emotions, and imagination), as well as cultural influences and past experiences, impact the decisions we make in life. We live in a dispensation in which *time* is more valuable than ever. One wrong decision can cost you years of your life, causing a timely detour from a preordained path that God intended for you to experience. Although no decision, *right* or *wrong*, is wasted (because "…all things work together for good to those who love God…" [Romans 8:28]), you can maximize your limited time on Earth as a productive citizen of the Kingdom of God by *understanding options* that lead to life-changing choices.

No form of knowledge can and will ever replace the direction and unction of the Holy Spirit. He is the Giver of true discernment. This information is to assist in understanding common scenarios, characteristics, the Word of God, etc., for a better understanding of "who is who" and "what is what" as it pertains to marriage. The enemy of mankind, known as Satan, wants to "rob" you of time and energy. His goal is to *influence* us to *choose* "*Counterfeit*" options as a strategy to get God's people off the course God has preordained for our lives. I can assure you that when you educate yourself with knowledge and wisdom from God through "the pen of a ready writer," the Holy Spirit will utilize and bring back to remembrance what you study and learn from this book during times of crucial decision-making.

My prayer is that this book helps you, ideally, to make Holy Spirit-driven *choices* in life to propel you into a prosperous future, to walk in purpose, and fulfill your *God-given* destiny. This is known as "the perfect Will of God." As we strive to become like our Savior Jesus, The Christ, the ultimate reward is hearing the words of our Lord Jesus: "Job well done, my good and faithful servant…" (Matthew 25:23).

CHAPTER One

CRITICAL DECISION-MAKING AREAS OF LIFE: MARRIAGE / SPOUSES, CAREERS, AND HOME REGIONS

The three most common areas and choices in life we both "hit the mark" and "hit the ball out of the ballpark"—or completely "miss the mark" and "strike out"—are pertaining to marriage, careers, and home regions/residency locations. The *right decisions* in these areas of life can *spare* us heartache, frustration, regret, negative drama, emotional scars and pain, loss of joy, wasted money and resources, and seemingly "wasted" time. The *right decisions* can *produce* satisfaction, an emotionally and mentally healthy state, joy, a sense of purpose and fulfillment, productivity, progressive goals, great stewardship of money, resources, and maximized time.

The five common types of *options*, which will be defined in detail in the chapters to follow, impact each of these areas: marriage, careers, and home regions/residency locations. The ultimate purpose of each area is to manifest God's plans on Earth through each of these avenues. Although we will find joy and satisfaction in these areas as we choose

His Will, the purpose of these avenues is not solely for our enjoyment. These are areas God utilizes to show forth His Glory and lead others to Eternal Salvation.

Whether you have a revelation of a deeper understanding of the importance of decisions or not, the one thing we all have in common (as a Believer in Christ or not) is we all want to "do the right thing"…make the "right choices"…and "avoid wasted time." All of these intentions seemly point back to one goal, whether you realize it or not: **to live out our lives in God's perfect Will.** As a result, we find ourselves in the pursuit of His Will, whether intentionally or unintentionally. We begin to commonly ask the following *crucial* questions as they pertain to the following areas of life:

Marriage:

The most common questions pertaining to marriage are the following:

- How do I *really* know he/she is "the One"?
- Did I hear God correctly regarding who is my mate?
- Why am I so drawn to this particular person?

Career:

The most common questions pertaining to career are the following:

- Is this the right career I should *really* invest my time in?
- Is this career a part of my purpose?
- Should I switch careers now and take a financial risk or remain financially stable although I was *drawn* to do something else?

Home Region:

The most common questions pertaining to home regions/residency locations are the following:

- ⚭ Should I relocate to a new city or state?
- ⚭ Should I move back to my hometown?
- ⚭ Why am I drawn to move to this new particular region?
- ⚭ Am I currently where I am supposed to be living?

Although there is no one answer to any of these questions that applies to **all** because everyone's story is different and unique, by the end of this book, hopefully you will have more insight regarding the various *options* who are potential mates that you encounter. And you can apply the process of elimination and cancel out "*Counterfeits.*" Most importantly, allow God to give you a *peaceful knowing* that serves as a confirmation to your "gut feeling" (the Holy Spirit) inside of you as you **conclude** what is *God's chosen desire* for you. This should lead to your next question....

*"Well...what **is** God's desire for me?"*

This is a great place to be, and speaking from experience, God honors your intention to know *His desire*. Why? Because it requires "delighting yourself in Him"! According to His Word, "He will bring *it* to pass!"

The experiential and revelational knowledge of this book was derived from the following scripture:

PSALM 37:4, ESV
Delight yourself in the L<small>ORD</small>*, and*
He will give you the desires of your heart.

God further gives us a guarantee in His Word that we WILL experience "the desires" through our ability to make the *right choices* that come from Him and as we *do our parts,* by stating in His Word... the very *next* scripture:

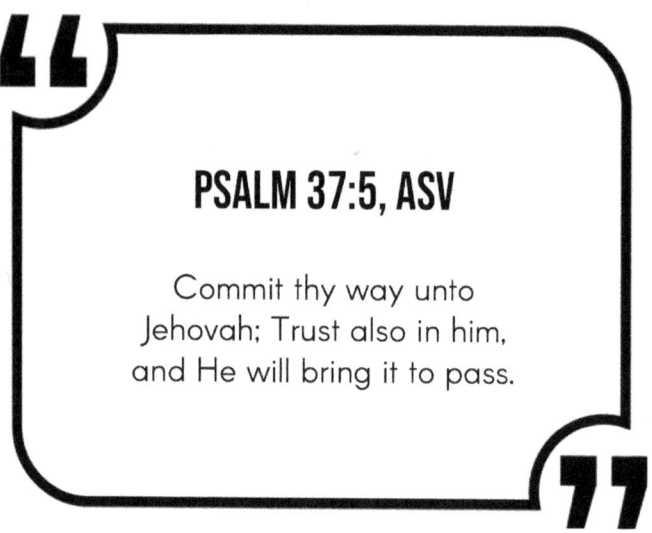

PSALM 37:5, ASV

Commit thy way unto Jehovah; Trust also in him, and He will bring it to pass.

"It" refers to "the desires" the Lord will *give* us and bring to pass. These "desires" still have to **become** our *choices.*

How this scripture applies to making choices will begin to *illuminate* and will make sense more and more as you continue reading.

Because this book is Biblically-based and Holy Spirit-driven, reading it is a form of delighting yourself in God by learning His ways. And soon enough, you will know what these "desires of your heart" are, given from God for your life without question or confusion.

The goal is to have a greater understanding of the *options* that present themselves throughout life and utilize the analogies and Biblical principles presented by applying them to any areas of life requiring critical decisions. Throughout the chapters, I will *briefly* point out and give examples of how understanding the *options* defined can clearly assist in other areas requiring major decisions. However, the primary focus of this book, *God's Divine Plans for Marriage* (Kingdom Choices–Marriage Edition, Book I), is to analyze our thought patterns as they pertain to marriage and mates and use the principles derived interchangeably.

CHAPTER Two

Defining "Wants" and "Needs"

There are **three main categories** and **three subcategories** that *choices* derive from when considering a mate, career, and residency.

The **main categories** are "*Wants,*" "*Needs,*" and "*Desires.*"

The **subcategories** are "*Likes,*" "*Neithers,*" and "*Counterfeits.*"

Although these categories are highly interchangeable with other areas of life, here are the definitions of *Wants* and *Needs* as they pertain to marriage.

Before we *dive* into the definitions of the various options we all face, understand the *options* we need to evaluate to decide on a mate, specifically, are different types of *human beings* that possess specific characteristics. Therefore, the categories *Wants, Needs, Desires,* etc., refer to *different types or groups of **people**, male or female,* who will fall into one of these categories when considering a mate.

The term "*Options*" refers to **ALL** categories of *people* because each type of person is an *option*. These *Options* create *choices*.

In addition, these are *also* the categories you may identify as *your* category and/or consider as another person's description.

Regardless of what you are seeking clarity for (whether it's the type of *Option* you are currently, another person's *Option* type, or both, *or something entirely different*), the *Option* types will become clear—to aid decisions and make personal adjustments. However, this discovery requires you to be very honest with yourself.

If there are two basic types, they are different and can't be the same; therefore, they are most likely opposite by definition. So let's analyze this theory of intrusive thought.

Definition of "Wants"

Wants are generally people you *like* and *think* you *need,* logically speaking. According to society's standards, they "fit the part" image-wise and are who you envisioned as a mate but do not have the rare qualities needed to specifically aid your uniqueness, especially over time. They have complementing qualities but are missing the essential qualities needed that are tailored for your individualism. They possess the qualities deemed "fit" according to one's familiarity, past *personal desires*, current *personal desires*, experiences, and even other people's opinions. These qualities satisfy the "now you" versus the "future you."

How Are "Wants" Created?

People become *Wants* by adopting a specific set of characteristics, behaviors, and mindsets over time, which are later described in detail. Ultimately, people **become** *Wants,* **attract** *Wants,* and are **attracted to** *Wants* because they appeal to our soul (mind, will, intellect, imagination, and emotions) through our psyche by the world's systems and subcultures. These systems consist of constant visual images (through TV, the Internet, social media, dating apps, advertisements, etc.) and cultural values, views, standards, etc. Our subcultures consist of the values, views, and opinions of family members and peers, religious/spiritual beliefs, and personal philosophies. These outlets have instilled beliefs of an "ideal" mate. Our way of life is formed according to what we are taught or choose (for ourselves) to accept as "truth" and ideal. This process begins at an early age during childhood. Our peers and circle of influence also contribute to what we consider our *wants* and shape our *personal desires*.

Definition of "Needs"

Needs are people you may not *want* initially but fulfill and complete the missing elements. They are not necessarily those at the top of the list of preferences. They are not who you envisioned as your mate, according to the surface, but they have the qualities and abilities you *need*. They possess something very special that is needed specifically for you that was put in them and developed, over time, as a rarity. These qualities are generally discovered through quality time and experienced behind closed doors, during one-on-one interaction, and rarely seen by the public eye. These mates have qualities that will be needed now and in the future and will adjust with you as time prevails.

How Are "Needs" Created?

The answer to this question is quite simple…NEW information and embracing the NEW! *Needs* are created through NEW knowledge, NEW information, NEW personal *transformation* through NEW obedience, and, most importantly, Biblical principles. You cannot become a *Need* without the **new** information that assists in governing your behaviors and perspectives. Hearing this *information* is a start, but hearing does not produce results. One must receive the information as "truth" and begin governing their actions accordingly through obedience to truth.

Personal *experience* can contribute to the understanding of *Need* characteristics but alone will not produce *Need* characteristics. Personal *transformation* is required to become a *Need*. The type of "transformation" I am referring to is when we deal with issues of the *soul*. It will uproot, eradicate, and expose erroneous beliefs, teachings, and mentalities so that the "new information" is **received**. As we build our *spirit man*, our *soul* must also receive *work* in the form of healing, strengthening, and purging. The end result of receiving *new information* as *truth* and implementing Biblical principles is…becoming a *Need*.

Please keep in mind…one *Option* type (*Want*, *Need*, etc.) is **not** better than the other. The *Option* type simply reflects one's current characteristics AND how one currently thinks. It reflects a moment in time. We are all going through a process and phases in life. Ideally, our behaviors and ways of thinking are constantly evolving at different paces.

There are clear characteristics that are prevalent to distinguish the difference between Wants and Needs (both female and male) discussed in the next section.

Common Differences of "Wants" and "Needs"

Wants and *Needs* are constantly mistaken for each other, hence the premise of this book. However, knowing the definitions of the two and how they differ, based on a distinct set of characteristics, will help you distinguish the difference and avoid *common mistakes*.

Here is a breakdown of how each category of **people** (referred to as "*Options*") operates, thinks, and behaves, generally speaking. Here are the common characteristics of *Wants* and *Needs* based on various topics.

"Wants" Versus "Needs" Topics:

Origin of Decision

Wants are driven by emotion, logic, and physical attraction. They are chosen by one who operates similarly, driven in this same manner.

Needs are driven by purpose, peace, and obedience. They are chosen by one who operates similarly, driven in this same manner.

Motives vs. Acceptance

Motives

Wants require (consciously or subconsciously) modifications and have hidden or ulterior motives to change another. The person of interest has value *but* needs to be tailored to fulfill certain *wants* or fantasies of an "ideal" mate.

Acceptance

Needs possess an element of acceptance of *what is*; the person of interest is accepted "*as is*" for who they are because they naturally fulfill the *needs*.

Confidence Levels

Wants are outwardly majorly confident, secretly insecure. They know they have the support of onlookers who see the logical "fit" for an ideal mate, creating an outward false confidence based on others' opinions. However, they are extremely aware that there is someone more suited to fulfill the other person's deeper *needs*, creating an inward insecurity.

Needs are outwardly confident, secretly even more confident and secure. They know they possess what the other person *needs* specifically and understand it is a matter of the other person's discovery, in time, to know the same. They are patiently aware that others will also agree in due time.

Planned Fantasy vs. God's Will / Open Heart

Planned Fantasy

Wants fixate on fantasies, usually preconceived/prior to meeting the person of interest. They attempt to shape and mold the other person's personality due to ulterior motives to match the interest to the fantasy. The person of interest becomes a "Fantasy Mate" versus a true "*Need*."

God's Will / Open Heart

Needs strongly desire God's Will with an *open* heart. They trust God enough to remain open-minded to accept whatever and whomever (*which* person of interest) He has granted His "stamp of approval." They do not possess preconceived ideas (regarding a person's personality and uniqueness).

<u>Titles</u>

Wants tend to question their position with the person of interest, which is usually self-proclaimed mentally. They prefer an official title ("Girlfriend" or "Boyfriend," "Hubby" or "Wifey") prematurely while dating and before marriage to limit the uncertainty—but are content with labeling *themselves* in their imaginations.

Needs are content in knowing who they are, simply "friend," "brother/sister in Christ," or "future mate" If revealed by God, and tend to avoid labels until the appointed time.

<u>"Paraders" vs. "The Focused"</u>

Paraders

Wants try to be seen with the intent to *become* an interest to another. This is in reference to the female *Want* only. Men are not "Paraders" for trying to be seen by a woman. Men, as the pursuers, must make themselves seen through some form of introduction but are not necessarily *Wants* as a result.

The Focused

Needs tend to draw people unintentionally. They don't initially know who they are drawing, when, and why. They are tunnel-focused on the task at hand and everyday life versus trying to be seen.

Self-Control

Wants lack self-control, which can apply to various areas, specifically, *physical desires* and hormones. Physical attraction is acted upon and, once unleashed, will do what it's going to do. You don't need to test it out. However, *Wants* allow curiosity to prematurely reveal (*so they think*) sexual compatibility or the lack thereof (*so they think*). They use the sexual experience as a determining factor to start, continue, or end a relationship.

This attraction is even more intense when the two are genuine friends. The intimacy possesses a unique passion felt from familiarity and understanding of the mate, manifesting in a more intense and passionate expression prematurely.

Most *Wants* who do not *want* to become physical convince themselves they can *trust* their flesh and control natural impulses, even in tempting circumstances.

Needs possess self-control by using *practical* wisdom. They are aware they cannot *trust* their flesh. Physical impulses are waited upon until the potential fulfillment of purpose is discovered, confirmed, and official (through marriage) to prevent disruption of purpose. The patience acquired to wait on exploring the natural physical attraction is due to wanting to do things God's way AND a strong interest in the unique qualities of the person of interest, which take time to be revealed. These unique qualities can also be camouflaged once other sexual interests are discovered.

Physical attraction is a natural instinct of both a *Want* and a *Need*. The absence of "*Need*" qualities met creates a void that requires a substitution (*another interest*) to develop any form of a relationship. A *Want* will substitute *lustful desires* for the lack of *needs* fulfilled, discovered, and/or demonstrated. This is because the sexual attraction outweighs other interests that are unmet or undiscovered.

God gives us the grace and ability to wait on sexual impulses, which is really what we *need*. In the meantime, one can be content discovering the other **interests** of a *Need*, which are suited for one's *needs* and purpose and outweigh the physical *wants*.

Function of the Heart vs. Protection of the Heart

Function of the Heart

Wants follow their heart, which eliminates boundaries verbally, physically, and emotionally (due to being *emotionally driven*).

Protection of the Heart

Needs guard their heart through choice words, controlled emotions, and physical boundaries (due to being *purpose-driven*).

Familiarity vs. Rarity

Familiarity

Wants possess qualities that are common/familiar (to one's experiences).

Rarity

Needs possess qualities that are rare (to one's experiences).

Anxiety vs. Contentment

Anxiety

Wants general attitude exudes "*pick me, pick me, pick me!*" Their persona exudes desperation, an impatient state of mind, and "needy."

Contentment

Needs general attitude exudes "*he/she can pick me or not.*" Their persona exudes confidence, convinced of high self-worth, and opposite of "needy."

Mediocre vs. Uniqueness

Mediocre

Wants possess qualities that can be *replaced*.

Uniqueness

Needs possess qualities that are *irreplaceable*.

Obsession vs. Preparation

Obsession

Wants become overly consumed with the thought of getting married or married to a specific person of interest. These thoughts are unmanaged and can lead to lustful acts in order to obtain the marriage through means of seduction. It can also lead to divorce if a decision to marry is derived from this state of mind.

Preparation

Needs become consumed with preparing themselves for a future mate by focusing on *being better* as individuals. The thoughts pertaining to marriage are managed because they are redirected into personal development as a goal…while waiting to obtain this *desire*.

Patience

Wants impress their *wants* (upon another). They create a plan for the development and progression of the relationship (journey or career path). They tend to believe anything contrary to *their* plan is an "ungodly" detour, creating an impatient state.

Needs discover *needs* (within another). They tend to believe the development and progression of a relationship (journey or career path) is not solely in their control. They understand planning is needed, but God can interrupt it at any given moment. There is a basic understanding that God's Will, which includes His timing, is perfect and acceptable, which produces patience.

Self-Delusion vs. Self-Awareness

Self-Delusion

Wants tend to convince *themselves* that they are *Needs* and who they *want* is a *Need*. They do not recognize reality. They are "blinded" by *wants* and *goals*. Also, due to their fixation on fantasy, they can want someone who does not want them or show *any* interest.

Self-Awareness

Needs are aware of the characteristics they possess, whether fully developed or underdeveloped. They understand no one is perfect. They are honest with themselves and where they "stand" regarding which *Option* type they are, as well as the *Option* types of others.

"Fall in Love" vs. "Discover Love"

Fall in Love

Wants seek to "fall in love" and develop deep emotions for the person of interest without a clear or proven objective for the relationship. They take emotional risks by developing strong feelings as a form of commitment to the relationship. As a result, they are prone to *soul ties* being mistaken for *love*. Physical looks also motivate their *personal desire* to develop strong feelings prematurely.

Discover Love

Needs seek to "discover love," which is to discover God in the relationship. Meaning, they look to see if God is the source, purpose, and origin of the relationship. The answer is evident to those with the mindset of a *Need*. It is not emotion-driven. In fact, emotions are not necessary during this phase. Discovering God's hand upon the relationship is the key factor, not feelings, emotions, financial stability, or even exterior looks. Looks may be used to attract the *Need's* attention but are not a strong enough factor, in itself, to keep the attention and interest of a *Need*.

Type of Being

Wants are codependent, internally *half*-beings. They are underdeveloped spiritually, emotionally, and mentally and immature in two or more of these areas.

Needs are self-sufficient, in a content state, and internally *whole*-beings. They are spiritually, mentally, and emotionally mature.

"Surface" Acknowledgment of God vs. True Relationship with God

"Surface" Acknowledgment of God

Wants demonstrate little to no acknowledgment of God—the Father God, the Holy Spirit, and Jesus, The Christ. He or she may reference God (in a social media post, for example), but will make little to no mention of Him in their daily life. This person may be a Believer (or not) who acknowledges God but does not appear to have a *relationship* with Him. Their relationship with God, or the lack thereof, is questionable and not clearly apparent through their lifestyle and/or conversation. They don't appear to depend on God. They can be a Believer, "Born Again," or "Saved" but *do not* demonstrate a fear of God. A true relationship with God is not evident.

True Relationship with God

Needs demonstrate a relationship with God—the Father God, the Holy Spirit, and Jesus, The Christ. They freely acknowledge Him consistently in conversations (and other means, such as social media posts, blogs, videos, etc.). They are a Believer, "Born Again," or "Saved" and genuinely *have* a fear of God. Their relationship with God is clear and evident through their lifestyle and conversation.

Summary Chart: The Different Characteristics of *Wants* and *Needs*

Different Characteristics of **"Wants"**		Different Characteristics of **"Needs"**
Origin of Decision Driven by emotion, logic, and physical attraction		**Origin of Decision** Driven by purpose, peace, and obedience
Motives Attempt to create the "ideal" mate through modifications to fulfill *wants*	vs.	**Acceptance** Accepts the person of interest "as is" who naturally fulfills needs
Confidence Levels Outwardly confident, secretly insecure		**Confidence Levels** Outwardly confident, secretly secure
Planned Fantasy Fixated on fantasy life and mates; mold person of interest to match the fantasy	vs.	**God's Will / Open Heart** No preconceived mate type; desire God's Will with an open heart to God's choice for a mate
Titles Prefer a label prematurely to aid insecurity		**Titles** Avoid labels until the appointed time
"Paraders" Try to be seen; refers to female *Wants* only	vs.	**"The Focused"** Draw people unintentionally; focus on life versus people; refers to male and female *Needs*

Different Characteristics of **"Wants"**		Different Characteristics of **"Needs"**
Self-Control Lack self-control, usually lack physical self-control; substitutes lust for unmet needs; put self first		**Self-Control** Possess self-control; do not trust flesh; needs discovered (possessed by the interest) outweigh physical wants; put God first
Function of the Heart *Follow* their heart; no boundaries; emotionally driven	vs.	**Protection of the Heart** *Guard* their heart; set up boundaries; purpose-driven
Familiarity Possess *common / familiar* qualities (and behaviors)	vs.	**Rarity** Possess *rare* qualities (and behaviors)
Anxious Exudes desperation and impatience; "needy" personality	vs.	**Contentment** Exudes confidence and patience; high self-worth; opposite of "needy"; can take or leave a new relationship
Mediocre Possess *replaceable* qualities	vs.	**Uniqueness** Possess *irreplaceable* qualities
Obsession Overly consumed with getting married and/or an interest; unmanaged thoughts regarding marriage and mates	vs.	**Preparation** Prepare for marriage through personal development; manage thoughts regarding marriage and mates

Different Characteristics of "Wants"		**Different Characteristics of "Needs"**
Patience Pace is impressed upon and dictated to the relationship according to one's *own* plans		**Patience** Cadence and pace of a relationship are discovered according to God's Will and timing
Self-Delusion Convinced they are *Needs* and any person of interest is also a *Need*; detached from reality; capable of wanting someone who does not want them or show interest	vs.	**Self-Awareness** Aware of their own characteristics— good or bad; honest about their own *Option* type; can assess others' *Option* type accurately
Fall in Love Seek to "fall in love" by developing strong emotional feelings prematurely without commitment; prone to "soul ties"	vs.	**Discover Love** Seek to "discover love" by discovering God in the relationship with or without commitment; non-emotional objective (initially)
Type of Being Co-dependent on others; internally *half*-beings; underdeveloped spiritually, emotionally, and mentally; immature		**Type of Being** Dependent on the Holy Spirit; internally *whole*-beings; developed spiritually, emotionally, and mentally; mature
"Surface" Acknowledgment of God Demonstrate *little* to *no* true *personal relationship* with God; do not fear God; relationship and dependency on God are not evident	vs.	**True Relationship with God** Demonstrate a true *personal relationship* with God that is apparent and consistent; fear God; relationship and dependency on God are evident

The Word of God says we will recognize others (specifically, false prophets) by their "fruit" (Matthew 7:16–20). We can utilize this Biblical principle to also *recognize* **anyone** and their character as well by observing the *fruit* they bear.

Those who are *Needs* demonstrate the "*fruit* of the Spirit": love, joy, peace, forbearance, kindness, goodness, faithfulness, gentleness, and self-control (Galatians 5:22–23). However, a person who is a *Want* can also appear to demonstrate these same attributes if he or she is skilled at creating appearance and perception to meet the *needs* of another once an understanding of another's *needs* is obtained. You will become highly skilled at discerning TRUE "fruit of the Spirit" as you learn to or become more skillful at recognizing *Counterfeits* and the *fruit* people *bear*.

Those with *Want* characteristics are in a stage in which they can be *wanted* but not *needed* by a person who is a *Need*. This is due to a lack of character and a need for more character development to reach the maturity level at which they *can be* needed.

Although *Wants* and *Needs* are fundamentally different, *character-wise*, they also have similar common characteristics and traits.

Some of the *Similar Characteristics* and Traits Between "Wants" and "Needs"

1. Both types attract their same type. *Needs* attract *Needs* and *Wants* attract *Wants*.
2. Both types tend to be on the same levels mentally, spiritually, and emotionally as another of the same type. *Needs* will be on the same maturity level (mentally, spiritually, and emotionally) as other *Needs*. *Wants* will be on the same maturity level (mentally, spiritually, and emotionally) as other *Wants*.
3. Both types make mistakes and will never be perfect beings.
4. Both types are undetectable according to appearance.
5. Both types are able to demonstrate authentic chemistry with another person.

Summary Chart: The *Similar* Characteristics of "*Wants*" and "*Needs*"

Common Characteristics of **"Wants"**	Common Characteristics of **"Needs"**
"*Wants*" attract "*Wants*"	"*Needs*" attract "*Needs*"
Similar mental, spiritual, and emotional **maturity levels** to the person of interest, but can also be drastically different	Similar mental, spiritual, and emotional **maturity levels** to the person of interest, but can also be drastically different (discussed later in Chapter 10)
Make mistakes; **imperfect**	Make mistakes; **imperfect**
Option type is **undetectable** according to appearance	**Option** type is **undetectable** according to appearance
Able to demonstrate authentic **chemistry** with another person	Able to demonstrate authentic **chemistry** with another person

A Mixture of "*Want*" and "*Need*" Characteristics

It is possible for someone to have a mixture of both "*Want*" and "*Need*" characteristics because becoming a *Need* is a process, simply put.

The difference between a Want and a Need is—a Want does not know or apply the beneficial alternative approach (God's ways) or mindset that directs behaviors.

Wants may know Godly, practical information, but until it is put into practice, it cannot become experiential knowledge that creates *Need* characteristics. Implementation is part of the true transformation process for permanent change but requires new knowledge plus time, effort, and exposure to God's Word. (*The first step is to repent—a true change of heart towards God.*)

For example, a person has heard information regarding setting boundaries to avoid the temptations of acting on *fleshly desires* but has not implemented it. As a result, they will portray the characteristics of a *Want* in the area of *self-control*, engaging in *fleshly desires*. Once the boundaries are continuously in **practice**, they will portray the characteristics of a *Need* in this particular area. This same person can demonstrate all other characteristics of a *Need* simultaneously. As a result, a mixture of *Want* and *Need* characteristics is portrayed.

When there is a mixture of characteristics, how do you know which Option type you are (or the person of interest is)?

When two or more *Want* characteristics are present, that person is considered a "*Want*."

If there is zero to one *Want* characteristic and the rest resemble a *Need*, that person is a *Need*. This person understands and has implemented God's requirements for conduct, mindsets, and disciplines. But because no one is perfect, faultless, or flawless, one area of *weakness* does not classify them as a *Want*. Due to their vast revelation in other areas, the *weakness* is most likely an area that demonstrates a *temporary moment(s) versus a lifestyle practice*. This *weak* area will change and transform due to their submission to the Lordship of Christ, leaving no gray areas unsubmitted.

So going back to the same example…if this person has demonstrated all characteristics of a *Need*, the lack of self-control *moment* will be just that…a *moment of weakness versus a continuous practice*. Therefore, in this example, the person would be considered a *Need*. Anyone who lacks self-control and engages in *fleshly desires* as a *continuous practice* will most likely have additional *Want* characteristics, equaling two or more, and therefore will be considered a *Want*.

Now that you have a basic understanding of the difference between "Wants" and "Needs," we can examine how each Option type differs as it relates to **gender** *and* **pursuit**.…

The Natural Male Pursuit Versus the Unnatural Female Pursuit

The Natural Male Pursuit

Men are designed to *naturally* seek the female *Needs* innately. There is a natural gravitation to *Needs* because the female mate is set in the path of a man to be seen and pursued to fulfill God's Will, if the man so *chooses*. A female *Want* is selected if the man falls into an impatient state to discover and explore the female *Need* because the *Need* is not always the *obvious mate* or *option*. Her qualities are revealed through quality time.

Needs

A **male** *Need* is aware he is a *Need* and will pursue a woman naturally. He will follow his inner witness out of curiosity and exclusively pursue a female *Need*, usually after the allotted time of close observation. Therefore, men *gravitate* to *Needs* when in a content state.

A **female** *Need* is aware she is a *Need*—and even when she is a *Need* to a *specific* man. However, she will demonstrate the opposite behavior of a male *Need*. She will NEVER pursue *any* man and prefers to be *discovered* as the *Need* and pursued.

Wants

A **male** *Want* is aware he is a *Want* and will pursue a woman naturally, as expected. His *initial* pursuit is similar to a male *Need*, and he *can* be mistaken as a *Need*. Therefore, it is much harder to recognize, initially, *some* male *Wants* from male *Needs*. They are considered *"Counterfeits"* (which will be discussed later in Chapter 6).

The Unnatural Female Pursuit

On the other hand, **female** *Wants* are *extremely* similar to male *Wants*. They are aware they are a *Want*. They also know when they are a *Want* to a particular man who shows interest directly or subtly; therefore, they will make themselves more available and/or known to the man and *pursue* him passively or aggressively. This is the "unnatural female pursuit."

In Conclusion...

It is important to keep a general understanding of the characteristics of each *Option* type, "*Wants*" and "*Needs*," as you continue to read this book.

These definitions serve as a basis as we build upon this understanding to learn how certain characteristics impact *choices* and behaviors that can lead us along God's plan or our *own*.

Chapter Three

The Origin of Solid Decision-Making: The Breakdown of Psalm 37:4

Before we can examine *the origin of solid decision-making*, let's first examine "solid decisions." Why is this important? It will take a *Godly solid decision* to marry the right person. So let's begin. There are two general definitions of *solid decisions*: one is according to the world's standards, and the other is according to God's standards—with worldly benefits.

Here are a few examples of *solid decisions* according to our society:

1. Going to college
2. Getting married between the ages of twenty-one and thirty
3. Having a baby with a person for financial wealth, whether married or unmarried
4. Accepting the highest-paying job
5. Moving in with a boyfriend/girlfriend or fiancé
6. Starting a business
7. Joining the army

This spectrum of examples includes multiple things in common, yet here are only a few similarities:

1. They all result from acting on a *choice*.
2. They all appear to benefit self at the least.
3. They derive from society's *taught* ideology for purposeful advancement.
4. They are not *solely* morally based.

These examples are not always deemed socially acceptable. The spectrum range has no clear moral indication. These **choices**/decisions can range from ethical to unethical, yet **the common denominator is self-advancement.**

So what makes a choice a Godly solid decision or a Worldly solid decision?

The answer is simple: the ***origin*** of the decision. The origin is either based on God's Will and *desire*, creating a *Godly solid decision*, or based solely on man's will, ambition, and *personal desire*, creating a *Worldly solid decision*.

Let's start with understanding Worldly solid decisions, which we all have made....

Worldly Solid Decisions

According to the world, "solid decisions" are self-centered. This type of decision-making is an act based on worldly benefits (not necessarily spiritual benefits) that appear sound and logical. It is the rationale we apply to the choice-making process taught by society to give one an advantage of some sort or propel one to progressive advancement.

In short, a *solid decision* according to the **world's standards** is self-advancement. This doesn't seem harmful... *until* you realize the fullness of the definition.

Worldly solid decisions are acts that lead to purposeful results and motive-driven *choices* for self-advancement...*by any means necessary.*

These *choices* are not based on *knowing* God's plans for one's life—but derive from *personal desire*. People are usually willing to do *anything* to manifest their decision.

Side note: Only what we do that God has us to do will *count.*

Godly Solid Decisions

The other type of "solid decisions" are *Godly solid decisions* according to **God's standards** but are **not** exclusive from the world's standards as well.

Godly solid decisions are acts that lead to fulfilling God's Will and purpose-driven choices based on knowing God's plan, instructions, and/or the Word of God.

The main difference between the two types of *solid decisions* is the *presence* or *absence* of God's Will in operation in one's life. God's Will *is* His Word constructed specifically for your unique path in life. *Godly solid decisions* are inclusive and a reflection of God's Will and are self-gratifying. Usually, part of the self-gratification is the benefit of others through this *type* of decision.

A *Godly solid decision* will be derived from a *choice* made from *knowing* exactly what God wants you to do based on a *desire* He *gives* you (Psalm 37:4). *"The steps of the righteous are ordered by the LORD"* (Psalm 37:23). It also derives from simply doing what God wants from a purely detected *Godly desire* from Him, not *always* realizing *who* or *what* is leading you or why. A logical question to ask at this point may be, *if you don't know if God is leading a decision, how do you know if it falls in this category (of "Godly solid decisions")?*

Godly solid decisions will NEVER contradict the Word of God. The more obvious distinction is the morally ethical or unethical aspect of a decision according to most people or society's standards. However, do not be deceived. Anything that God did not ***instruct*** us to do, even if it seems ethical and *harmless,* will not count as obedience and advance His Kingdom. He will *allow* the decisions (due to free will), but they will not reflect the life He preordained for you.

> **PROVERBS 16:20, NIV**
>
> Whoever gives heed to instructions prospers, and blessed is the one who trusts in the Lord.

This is not to say *worldly solid decisions* are not useful. God has allowed us to make them (through our free will) to lead up to a lesson that brings us closer to Him. The Bible states "…all things work together for good to them that *love* God, to them who are called according to *his* purpose" (Romans 8:28, KJV). This love starts with a decision to accept Jesus, The Christ as your **Savior** (to keep you saved and connected to God). Jesus said "…I am the way, the truth, and the life. No one comes to the Father except through Me" (John 14:6).

In addition, you must *also* accept Jesus as your LORD so He can begin to "direct your path" (Proverbs 3:6). (The results of our decisions are discussed more in Chapter 14.) So in order to truly make *Godly solid decisions*, we must *first* love God and submit to Jesus, The Christ. *Godly solid decisions* are driven by obedience **and** discipline. There will always be a spiritual benefit, yet the common benefit is God's Glory in the testimony due to obedience.

The Benefits of Godly Solid Decisions

Here are a few examples of *Godly solid decisions* with **spiritual benefits** in *conjunction* with **worldly benefits** deemed socially acceptable, to say the least, from the previous list of examples.

These examples can *also* be used to understand the highest form of deception (if God did not instruct them) because they seem *harmless* and *good*.

1. Going to college

   - The **Spiritual Benefits**: The testimony that glorifies God, more open doors according to God's Will/plans for your life as a result, and awareness of self

   - The **Worldly Benefits**: If God directs you to go—an earned degree, credibility as a "finisher," one who values education, and the education itself received

2. Getting married…at the age which God leads you to this decision, according to purpose, with an understanding of marriage, His Will, and timing

   - The **Spiritual Benefits**: The testimony that glorifies God, the advancement of His Kingdom by *hitting the ground running* as a *solid* couple *equally yoked*, sexual intimacy, reproduction, DOMINION (primarily), *spiritually* deemed "complete" (Genesis 1:27–28), etc.

   - The **Worldly Benefits**: Marital perks such as tax breaks, discounts, etc.; *socially* deemed "complete"; joint financial responsibilities and/or financial benefits, etc.

3. Accepting the highest-paying job as the Lord directs you

   - The **Spiritual Benefits**: The testimony that glorifies God, in God's Will (doing what God wants you to do, being in the place and position God wants you to be in), the opportunity to advance the Kingdom of God through financial giving, keeping the corporation *afloat*, being a "light" as a moral soundboard, etc.

   - The **Worldly Benefits**: Financial gain, respect from the general society, materialism, appeal to the opposite sex

Now that we have an understanding of the two distinct *types* of solid decisions, *Worldly* and *Godly*, we can *now* trace the origin of both for a greater understanding.

The Origins:

- 💍 ***Worldly solid decisions***: The origin is a self-centered nature influenced by society, culture, experiences, and family backgrounds—to benefit *self*, without knowledge of God's leading.

- 💍 ***Godly solid decisions***: The origin is God's Will according to knowledge influenced by the Word of God, His directions and instructions, and prayer—to benefit *self*, *others*, and the Kingdom of God.

So what can we conclude?

The Word of God is designed to help our decision-making process. It is a guide for our thinking.

The origin of **all** solid decisions will always be based on how we view life and where we are in life—spiritually, mentally, and emotionally. It is a byproduct of our soul (mind, intellect, will, imagination, and emotions) *or* our spirit (including our mind, body, and soul).

Now let's take it a little deeper…. **The source of the origin is either God, yourself, other people, or humanity's adversary, Satan.** This is partially the reason why the Word of God instructs us to "renew our **mind**." This ACTION results in "His good, acceptable, and perfect Will" (Romans 12:2) derived from *Godly solid decisions* due to obedience!

The Ultimate Self-Check & Reference "Tool"

Here is a guide and a few scriptures that will always lead us to make a *Godly solid decision* according to knowledge and understanding that will align with His Will…and keep us safe in His Will:

 **Manage every thought.**

> **PHILIPPIANS 4:8, NIV**
>
> Finally, brothers and sisters, whatever is true, whatever is noble, whatever is right, whatever is pure, whatever is lovely, whatever is admirable—if anything is excellent or praiseworthy—think about such things.

*This will always **guide** our thinking and emotions in the right direction.*

> **2 CORINTHIANS 10:5, ESV**
>
> We destroy arguments and every lofty opinion raised against the knowledge of God, and take every thought captive to obey Christ...

*This **prevents** us from receiving corruptible "seeds" (negative words spoken about us, to us, against us or the Word of God) that produce a negative harvest if left unchecked.*

⚭ **Trust God.**

> **PROVERBS 3:5-6, NAS**
>
> Trust in the LORD with all your heart and do not lean on your own understanding. 6. In all your ways acknowledge Him, and He will make your paths straight.

*Trusting in the Lord wholeheartedly instead of our own understanding, which is limited, will **aid our decisions** towards God's Will for us. If we acknowledge the Lord in all we do, think, consider, etc., He will "direct" our "paths," as Proverbs 3:6 NKJV states. The Holy Spirit will **guide** us.*

⚭ **Use the Word of God to live and to *check* motives (three versions of this scripture for understanding).**

> **HEBREWS 4:12, NLT**
>
> For the word of God is alive and powerful. It is sharper than the sharpest two-edged sword, cutting between soul and spirit, between joint and marrow. It exposes our innermost thoughts and desires.

HEBREWS 4:12, ESV

For the word of God is living and active, sharper than any two-edged sword, piercing to the division of soul and of spirit, of joints and of marrow, and discerning the thoughts and intentions of the heart.

HEBREWS 4:12, NIV

For the word of God is alive and active. Sharper than any double-edged sword, it penetrates even to dividing soul and spirit, joints and marrow; it judges the thoughts and attitudes of the heart.

Our decisions are a byproduct of our thoughts driven by our soul (mind, will, intellect, imagination, emotions) **or** *our spirit (inclusive of our mind, body, and soul). Only the Word of God can* **reveal** *to us the source. In addition, the Word of God will also reveal our own motives to self.*

⚭ **Identify the true adversary (three versions of this scripture for understanding).**

> ### EPHESIANS 6:12, NKJV
>
> For we do not wrestle against flesh and blood, but against principalities, against powers, against the rulers of the darkness of this age, against spiritual hosts of wickedness in the heavenly places.

> ### EPHESIANS 6:12, NLT
>
> For we are not fighting against flesh-and-blood enemies, but against evil rulers and authorities of the unseen world, against mighty powers in this dark world, and against evil spirits in the heavenly places.

EPHESIANS 6:12, NIV

For our struggle is not against flesh and blood, but against the rulers, against the authorities, against the powers of this dark world and against the spiritual forces of evil in the heavenly realms.

*Again, the **source** of the origin of solid decision-making is either God, yourself, other people, or humanity's adversary, Satan. It is important to know **who and what is driving a choice** so we don't make decisions that can derail us from His Will. We also don't want to go against or attack the wrong source. This is why it is imperative to know "who's who" and "what's what" when making choices.*

In Conclusion…

The origin of all *solid decisions* will always be based on how we view life and where we are in life—spiritually, mentally, and emotionally. Underdevelopment in these areas will result in *worldly solid decisions*. Intentional development in these areas will result in *Godly solid decisions*.

The final scripture that will always reveal to us the origin and source of a *desire* is Psalm 37:4….

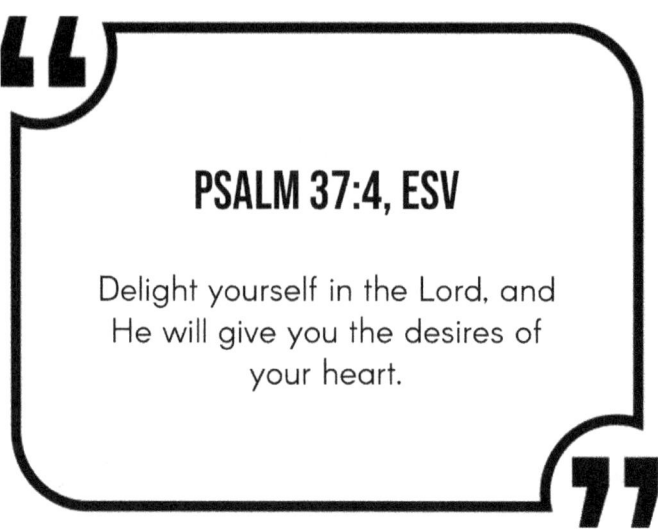

"PSALM 37:4, ESV

Delight yourself in the Lord, and He will give you the desires of your heart."

If we are delighting ourselves in the Lord, "the desires" will be **from** Him. They will originate from Him. He will be the source.

God further gives us a guarantee in His Word that we WILL experience "the desires" He *gives* through our ability to make the *right choices* that come from Him and as we do our parts—by stating in His Word:

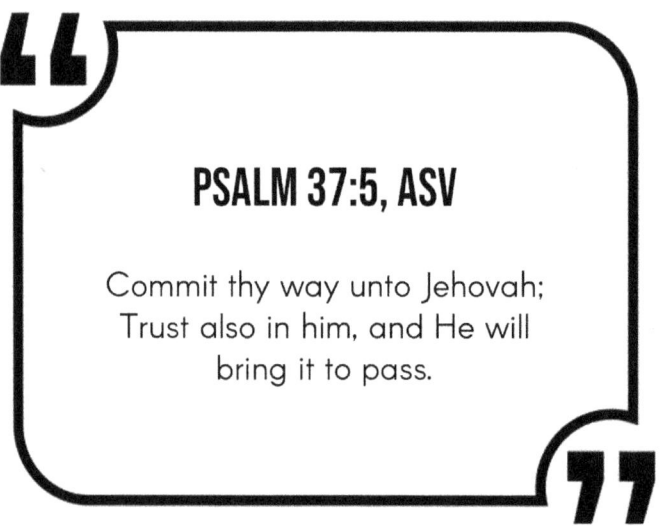

"PSALM 37:5, ASV

Commit thy way unto Jehovah; Trust also in him, and He will bring it to pass."

OUR part is to "delight" ourselves "in the Lord" (Psalm 37:4) and "commit our ways" to Him and "trust Him" (Psalm 37:5).

What *desires* are you experiencing that are not necessarily from your personal, learned preferences and do not contradict the Word of God?

This is a **strong indicator** of a possible *desire* from God *given* to you and placed in your heart. What and whom **He gives us** is what and whom we are fully equipped to handle if received by *choice*. Another strong indicator of a *desire* from God is PEACE. God will put the "desire" in your heart for the person, place, or thing He wants you to have, and it **will** come with extreme peace. If you are not experiencing a very tangible peace, ***do not*** make any decisions. **Be patient.**

CHAPTER *Four*

THE DEFINITION OF "DESIRES": INTRO TO "NEEDED WANTS" A.K.A. GOD'S DESIRES

Those who find themselves in the perfect Will of God for marriage usually experience a very common journey *before* marriage. They transition from those who are *"Wants"*...to maturing to those who are *"Needs"*...to becoming *"Needed Wants,"* who are **also** *"Desires."* The final destination of becoming a *Desire* is established once the "self-work" reaches an acceptable level **according to Christ**.

So how does a person who is a *Need* become a *Needed Want / Desire?* It is through a process of discovery described in this next section.

The "Desire" Discovery Process: Transition from "Need" to "Needed Want"

Prior to one knowing, thinking, and doing things God's way, we start off as *Wants*. We are in pursuit of achieving a goal, relationship, etc., our *own* way due to learned behavior and the influence of culture, society, family, friends, teachers, mentors, etc. Religion and ministries may even influence some to do things their *own* way—if unknowingly mistaught to follow *man* over God. Once we begin to adapt to God's way of doing things, renewing our minds and changing our behavior to resemble Christ, we mature from a *Want* into a *Need*. However, the focus of this chapter is the transition from one being a *Need* to **becoming** a *Needed Want / Desire*.

Needs aren't originally who we tend to *want* because those who are *Wants* get most of our attention (depending on our mindset and patience). This occurs when we are unaware of the Godly characteristics to look for. As discussed previously in Chapter 2 (Defining "*Wants*" and "*Needs*"), *Wants* resemble **our** *own plans* for ourselves, what we tend to *like* and *want,* and our *preconditioned desired* qualities.

However, in time, those who are *Needs* become *wanted* for very similar reasons because they resemble **not** necessarily our *own plans* per se—but **God's plans** for our lives as well as *Need* characteristics. They resemble our **NEW** *likes,* one or more qualities we originally *wanted,* and a **NEW** *Godly desire* and attraction to Christ-like, **Godly qualities**.

These *Godly desires* are *given* to us and implanted in our hearts by God Himself as we delight in Him according to Psalm 37:4. God's *desires,* now in *our* hearts, become *our desires* and resemble His perfect Will.

This process is how we begin to desire what He desires for us. As we adopt God's ways of thinking and HIS "*desires*" are **accepted**, the one who is a *Need* becomes a "*Needed Want*"—who we *need and want,* in short.

This is how a *Need* transitions to a *Needed Want* who is also a *Desire* (God's *chosen* spouse for you), hence the term, *Needed Want / Desire*. The transition is complete once *God's desire* is discovered and accepted.

No *Option* (person) will top *God's desire (Desire)*, His choice for you. However, many people will miss this blessing (until it comes around again, if ever) by **not accepting** *God's desire (Desire)* and plan.

The great news is…there is a way to **avoid** this time-costly mistake described in the next section.

Prerequisites to *Accept* a "Need" as a "Needed Want" / "Desire"

It is not enough to be able to recognize a person who is a *Need*. You must also *accept* a *Need*. In order to *receive* and *accept* the *Need* (and experience the *Need* becoming a *Needed Want / Desire*), there are a few **prerequisites** one must acquire that will lead to a POWERFUL *choice* for a mate. This *choice* will produce a POWERFUL marriage that will *hit the ground running* for God's Kingdom.

The First Prerequisite: Self-Worth

The first prerequisite is to change our mindset and focus **from** our *preconditioned desires* for ourselves (defined by others and society) **to** *Godly desires* for ourselves (defined by God). This means you must possess a *Godly desire* for your self-worth, self-knowledge, self-image, and Kingdom value, which is your *true self-value*. As a result, you will *desire* to discover and resemble the "true you." (Understand, *true self-value* is not the same as your value defined by society's standards, which denotes self-esteem.)

Once you *desire* to resemble the *true you*—you are one step closer to (1) **becoming** a *Need* yourself (character-wise), (2) **attracting** another who is also a *Need*, and (3) being able to **accept** the *Need* God will give you a *desire* for in time.

A *desire* to work on yourself leads to the actual work required and accomplished. As the old saying goes, *"Where there is a will, there is a way."* As you *will (choose)* to transform into one who is a *Need*, the *way* will be illuminated and recognized.

The Second Prerequisite: The "Open Heart"

The second prerequisite is to have an "open heart" without seeing the full story. Having an *open heart* is simply being open to *God's Will, His plans*, and *whatever* He wants to do with your life. God knows exactly what you *need* and *want* in a mate. Yet a strong appeal to the mate He chose is not always immediately recognizable. Instead, it is "discovered" over time. He or she (or "it," such as an opportunity) may not *look like* or *seem like* what you envisioned, although you recognize the qualities and potential for partnership. **Openheartedness** is **key** to *recognizing*, *receiving*, and *accepting* the person who is a *Need*.

You must get rid of "the list" of things that don't matter that keeps your heart closed to God's perfect Will.

<u>The Third Prerequisite: Trusting God</u>

The third prerequisite is trusting God. You must trust God with the "desire" He *gives* you (based on Psalm 37:4) *without* seeing the full story and *without* evidence in the natural. This is the essence of pure and true *faith*.

Trusting God requires faith in the *present* moment. "***Now*** faith is the substance of things hoped for, the evidence of things not seen" (Hebrews 11:1, KJV). Having "faith" ***now***, in the present moment, is a result of ***trusting* God *now…not later…not based on our own timeline and plans…and not based on what we see or don't see.*** And it produces confidence in God's Word, promises, and plans…***right now.*** This allows you to accept the person God gives you a desire for within the allotted "window" of time because of your present faith.

When you have "faith," your Kingdom spouse is the "substance," one who already exists, and whom you must have "hope" for. "Faith" is *also* the actual "evidence" or proof of who was created—who is not visible. This understanding is vital to accepting the person God has chosen for you. Without faith, the person will not exist because of a lack of hope that causes you not to accept them when met. The "evidence" of this person's existence who is not *seen (spiritually and figuratively speaking)* will not exist.

In addition, the Word of God gives a *guarantee* as it pertains to trust: "Whoever gives heed to instructions prospers, and **blessed** is the one who **trusts** in the L<small>ORD</small>" (Proverbs 16:20, NIV). **It takes trust to follow instructions.**

Accepting the person God gives you a "desire" for is one of those instructions.

Trusting God is key to ***recognizing***, ***receiving***, and ***accepting*** the person who is a *Need*.

The Fourth Prerequisite: Be a "Need"

You, yourself, must be a person who is a *Need*, character-wise. Remember, *Needs* attract *Needs*, simply put.

The Transition from "Need" to "Needed Want" / "Desire"

Now that we understand what is required of us to *receive* and *accept* the person who is a *Need* as a *"desire"* from God, He can *reveal* to us a specific *Need* who becomes a *Needed Want / Desire*.

God is waiting to **reveal** to us **what** we *need*, requiring us to seek Him first (Matthew 6:33) and delight in Him (Psalm 37:4). Next, God is waiting to **reveal** to us **who** we *need* in the form of a heart's "desire" (Psalm 37:4) for a person.

Delighting in the Lord **allows** you to ***recognize*** and ***discover*** the *Needed Want / Desire* as you spend time basking in His presence. He will *reveal* to you the *"desire"* He placed in *"your heart"* before you were born, before the beginning of time. Most importantly, you must act on the instruction. Once you act on and *manifest* a step (through belief, trust, faith, and obedience), the next step will be *revealed*. This is the same process when God framed the world in Genesis (Genesis 1:1–2:1).

Delighting in the Lord also ***reveals*** the Lord's *preordained desires* of our hearts, which are also who and what we *need* as individuals and to advance God's Kingdom; this includes a specific mate. The *preordained desire* is implanted in our hearts for us to ***recognize*** in His timing. *Why?* He is a God of protection and satisfaction. He will protect us (even from what we cannot see) and give us an abundant life full of purpose, satisfaction, wisdom, and joy. Therefore, the timing He chose in advance to reveal His *desires* is to protect us from aborting His plans. Remember, God's Timing is "good, acceptable, and perfect" because it's a part of His Will.

Once a *Need* is **revealed, recognized, discovered, received, and accepted,** the *Need* NOW becomes the *Needed Want / Desire,* who produces a true and *healthy desire* because it comes from God.

Understanding God's Will Pertaining to Our Wants and Needs

God made us. He knows what we *want* that will not harm us. Most people aren't in tune or aware that *some* attributes we *want* are by design for a greater purpose. And *some* attributes we *want* in another can be harmful.

God also knows what we *need*. Those *needs* are discovered as we discover our true selves (that resemble Jesus, The Christ) and our *God-given* purpose in life. Without this discovery, what we think we need is usually inaccurate, and the understanding is not fully developed.

Who God has for us will possess harmless attributes we *want* and strong attributes we *need*. Therefore, the *Needed Want* is the *Desire* **God** gives us in our hearts, referred to as a *Needed Want / Desire*. This person possesses what we want and need **and** is a *desire* given to us by God. The *healthy desire* always begins after the discovery (which is confirmation) that he or she (or "it," such as an opportunity) is from God.

Forget about what you think you *want* and *need* ("…lean not on your own understanding…"); recognize God *is* the *One* in control ("…acknowledge Him…") so He can lead you ("…He will direct your path…" Proverbs 3:5–6) to **discover** your healthy wants and needs and the person who is the *Needed Want / Desire* from Him! JESUS!

To come to the place where we experience life with our *Needed Want / Desire* is our ultimate goal. *Needing who and what* we *want* is a preference. Ideally, we should *desire who and what* we *need*. But we must also *want who and what* we *need*, or we'll reject them or it. Most *fall short* by **not** *wanting* who they actually *need*, the *right person* (place or thing). This is due to the strategies of the enemy who does not want people to experience God's best for their lives, which is God's Will, and the *Need* He preordained.

Wanting the *Need* isn't always immediate and automatic if you quickly advance to adapting God's ways. In this case, the person may flat out not be the type you're used to. As a result, you may not *see* God in the situation immediately. But when it is God and you invest time getting to know the person, you will discover qualities and personality traits you'll *want* as well as *need*.

Seeing the *Need* for who they are, as God's chosen *Desire* for you, makes it **easy** to *want* and *need* them for your Kingdom marriage, to experience God's best, and to fulfill life's purpose as God ordained.

We must *accept* the one who is the *Desire*. Once God *gives* you and reveals the *"desire,"* then and only then can you *choose* the **right** Godly desire (*Desire*) through your free will.

I want to make this step *extremely* clear, which is based on very specific circumstances. You can accept a *Needed Want / Desire* once revealed WITHOUT the other person being aware of the revelation God has *given* to you. God is in control of the timing in which both *Needs* will become aware of being *Desires* to each other (discussed in detail later in Chapter 10, "Timing and Windows…").

Lastly, the *Need* of *interest* becomes a *Needed Want / Desire* once you **choose** to accept the **person** as God's Will for marriage, which is the "desire" God *gives* you. If God *gives* it to *you*, that means you can *choose* to accept what He gives you—or not. God's Will is never automatic. It always **requires** acceptance on our part; otherwise, He is violating His own law of *free will*.

Important Step

After both *Needs* become *Desires* to each other, they are aware of each other as such, and both feel the leading of the Holy Spirit, they can *choose* to proceed to the Discovering Love phase of the "Discovery of Love" process (discussed later in Chapter 8). If they *choose* to proceed and advance the relationship, it is crucial for BOTH parties to seek spiritual guidance (i.e., Christ-led, trustworthy pastor) for a credible witness, accountability, and wise counsel. Each person should be transparent, honest, and straightforward regarding the intent of the relationship.

Identifying *God-Given* "Desires" (People)

Let's examine **how** to identify those who are *God-given Desires* using an everyday scenario:

Two Women Want the Same Man

If two women *want* or *desire* (in their hearts) the same man, did God purpose this man to be with both? No. So who *gets* the man? The woman whom **God** *gave* the man the *innate desire* to **pursue** exclusively. She is the *God-given Desire*. A CLEAR GIVEAWAY to know which woman is **NOT** the *God-given Desire* is the woman who pursues the man. This pursuit is NOT in the Will of God for his life (or her life) as it pertains to marriage.

Key to Remember

Who and what people can consider "desires" are not always given by God. There are many types of desires, such as personal desires, lustful desires, innate desires, Godly desires, soul desires, fleshly desires, secret desires, worldly desires, carnal desires, pleasure desires (James 4:1), etc.

God is a God of order. The order He ordained can be found in His Word regarding marriage. His Word says, "…he that *finds* a wife finds a good thing…" (Proverbs 18:22). The man will always find the woman/

wife when she is from God. However, there is only one Holy Spirit. If the Holy Spirit gives the man (as the pursuer) a *desire* for the woman, He will also give the woman (as the one pursued) a *desire* for the man.

It can be around the same time or at different times. This man will be **Holy Spirit-led** and **purpose-driven**. And both life purposes will *align* and work together to establish *Dominion*. This is why God gave the woman a *Godly desire* for him, and the man a *Godly desire* for her.

Key to Understand

When God gives you a desire for someone, it comes with patience and confidence. Why? Because God gave him or her to you. It will always come with a sense of peace.

God's Will is peaceful. Confusion should not be prevalent.

…**Unless**, in some cases, there is a demonic spirit working against HIS Will through division and deception. And if so, this is a clear indication of a very **powerful** marriage. If the demonic strategy is recognized and does not detour them from marriage with each other, they will do **extremely great works for Jesus**. Remember, the enemy will use what he can based on your weakness.

When two interests are *Needs*, and you are unsure of who may be for you, limit the communication with the one of *lesser* interest (for example, to public settings only or in passing during natural opportunities). Make sure you verbally make it clear you are simply looking for a friend to establish a friendship *before* a possible romance. In the meantime, continue looking to "discover love"/God in the other friendship of stronger interest. (A chart and a more detailed guide is provided later in Chapter 13.)

One thing I have learned…"***There is only one Holy Spirit!***" His instructions to one will coincide with His instructions to another who hears and obeys the Lord. His instructions are never contradictory. For example, suppose He is telling you to *limit your interaction* with one. In that case, He is also telling the other person the same thing to avoid unintentional feelings of *rejection* due to mere obedience. This is an indication there is an appointed time for a *new* instruction to either **increase interaction** according to God's perfect timing (Romans 12:2), or **decrease interaction**, or **cease interaction** indefinitely. Timing is a part of His perfect Will.

Now let's examine **how** to identify those who are *God-given Desires* using a Biblical scenario from 1 Kings 3:16–28:

Two Women "Desire" the Same Baby

In this story, two women were claiming to be the biological mother of the same baby. The women were put to the test by King Solomon. He threatened to cut the baby in half and give a part to each woman. The *real* mother spoke up and relinquished her rights to the child to the other woman versus her infant child experiencing such a gruesome death. The *Counterfeit* (discussed in a later chapter)/false mother agreed with the child being put to death. The baby was "spared" by King Solomon and given to the real mother because of her motherly love that was instantly revealed. The real mother had a *God-given* "desire" to love the child. The *Counterfeit* "mother" did not have a *Godly desire* for the child.

In Conclusion…

There is generally a process to receive *everything*, both "good" and "bad" things. This process can be intentional or unintentional. However, each type of process can work for your benefit or your demise.

The **great news** is you have a *choice*! You can *choose* to initiate a process that will benefit your life. *Choosing* to obtain *God's desire* for your life initiates the process that can lead to God's perfect Will. Once you are able to recognize and acknowledge a person who is a *Need*, you have begun the transition that leads to the revealing of **God's desire** for you! Once you have accepted God's *Desire*, you are on your way to experiencing a Kingdom marriage!

Chapter *Five*

The Danger of Misinterpreting Psalm 37:4

We live in an era in which false doctrine and misinterpretations of scriptures can flood the airwaves through social media, satellite radio, the Internet, and some pulpits through online church services—becoming more and more accessible and acceptable by others unable to discern erroneous teachings. Many scriptures are misinterpreted. But there is one, *if* taught incorrectly or misunderstood, will cause people to live their lives in search of what "feels right" to their spirit *so they think* (and their flesh unknowingly) *or* apply faith to the wrong things…. In *actuality*, they are searching for what "feels right" to their *soul* and will use ANYTHING to confirm this *feeling*, including scriptures.

Understanding the information in this chapter will help you *choose* the right suitable mate God has for you—and ***avoid*** self-deception (specifically when relying on the interpretation of the Word of God) and seeking your will over God's Will (knowingly or unknowingly).

The Misuse of Psalm 37:4

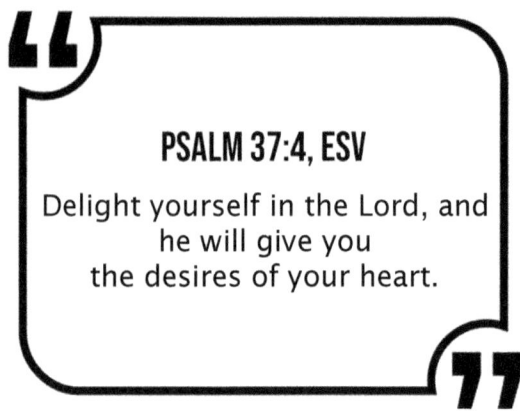

> **PSALM 37:4, ESV**
> Delight yourself in the Lord, and he will give you the desires of your heart.

This scripture is commonly misinterpreted to believe "desires" refers to *our wants* and the secret things we *want* in our hearts. It is also commonly believed the word "desires" refers to our *personal desires* that God "grants" us. If this is the interpretation, one will **believe** that people, places, things, and opportunities we *want* and actually *receive* are **all** from God—but they're not. All of what and whom we *want* is not motivated by God. The *desires* that are not from God are derived from the *influences* of various sources other than directly from God. Just because you have a *desire* for something, *want,* or even *need* something or someone does not mean that God agrees you should have it (or them) and is a *desire* from Him.

The misinterpretation of this scripture is perceived as—the person, place, or thing we *want*, believe we *need*, or *personally desire* in our heart is what God *will* **give** us as long as we "delight" in Him. **This is the misconception.** God does not give us *our desires* because *our desires* are tainted and not in line with His Will. They are the result of various secular, soulical, and social influences. Instead, God *gives* us HIS "desires" by first implanting them in our "hearts" according to His Will. Then and only then will *our desires* align with His Will for our lives. **Knowing God's Will for you *is* knowing His "desires" for you.**

As discussed in Chapter 4 of this book, these *desires*—in reference to *people*—are referred to as *Needed Wants / Desires,* also known as *Godly desires*.

With this understanding, now **re-read** Psalm 37:4:

"Delight yourself in the LORD, and **he will give you** the **desires of your heart.**"

Make sense? This scripture is now illuminated through revelation and understanding. GOD GIVES DESIRES! The *desires* God gives us are far GREATER than our own. His *desires* create our destinies…and result in DOMINION.

Let's examine a few hypothetical scenarios:

Scenario One:

A woman who admired and looked up to great financial providers and protectors while growing up may *desire* a man who is a drug dealer. It is not a *bad thing* according to the customs of her subculture. She begins to "delight" herself in the Lord, seeking Him and spending time with Him to the best of her knowledge. She interprets Psalm 37:4 as a scripture that God proposes to give us what *we desire* in our hearts as we "delight" in Him. So she asks God to *give* her the *desire* of her heart: a man who is a successful criminal with wealth, a protector, and a great father. This is *her personal desire* and, subsequently, what she asks God to *grant*. God will not give her this *desire*. He *gives* "desires" according to His Will. First John 5:14 states, "And this is the confidence we have before Him, **if we ask anything according to *His Will*, He hears us**." He does not just grant *our desires* if it is NOT *His Will* or because we prayed for it. We can *choose* our *own desires* (through free will), **but** that is *our will* in place, **not** His.

However, if she ends up with him, she may believe the relationship is an answered prayer and stay in a situation that was not God's plan for her life. What keeps people *stuck* (outside of God's Will) is their *own faith (for their own will and plans)* working against them, believing a situation was God's doing (orchestration) but was not. This is not to say God cannot bless a union made between a woman and a man who dealt drugs for a living…but IF this is his current lifestyle, it would not be God's Timing to initiate the covenant to make him the woman's spiritual covering/husband at *this* time, therefore not His Will. (God's Will includes timing.)

Scenario Two:

A man *desires* a wife…a Godly woman with no kids, with a great-paying job, and who is a devout Christian within the child-bearing age, preferably early thirties. This is *his desire* in his heart. He interprets Psalm 37:4, as many do, to believe God will give him this *desire* of *his* heart. No scripture forbids any of *his desires*. His *desire* seems to *appear* to align with *Godly desires* or what could possibly be considered God's Will…. *But does it really?* God knows what we *need* and *want* long term. As the man *lets go* of *preconditioned desires* with an open heart, he prays for God's Will while working on self (as *Needs* do). As a result, he **receives** a *desire* for a woman in her mid-thirties with two kids and a heart for Christ. She is a homemaker with a business plan in the works/beginning stages. This is the woman God *gives* him a *Godly desire* to pursue. It is unexplainable…even *not* who or what he envisioned. Yet he is full of joy and tangible peace.

Scenario Three:

Lady A is thirty-two years old and ready for marriage. She *wants* or prefers a man who has never been married, so she doesn't consider divorced men an *option* for marriage. However, God knows what she *needs* and how her thoughts will change with more knowledge, experience, respect for time, and the discovery of her purpose. By the time Lady A is thirty-eight, due to her maturity level, her inexperience in marriage, and her purpose, God knows she *needs* a divorced man of God to bring a certain level of experiential relationship knowledge to the table to avoid timely newlywed mistakes due to *both* parties being inexperienced (regarding a healthy marriage). He may need to have some form of knowledge to add value and aid her purpose and their purpose together, producing a complementary element of ministry. She, *unknowingly*, is called to minister to broken women; and he, *unknowingly*, is called to minister to broken men who experienced one or more *"failed"* marriages. As God's Will/assignment is revealed in time, the Holy Spirit orchestrates their paths to cross, and God *gives* them a *Godly desire* for each other. He pursues…she accepts… **DOMINION** on Earth increases.

Life is funny. We all know what we *want*, generally speaking, but we seldom *really* know what we *need,* especially in time…later in life…long term…and in the future.

A Pastor's Story

A very honorable minister of five years, at the time, was a divorced man of God with four young children, living with his parents. He knew he was called to be a pastor and began pastoring a small Bible study group. He wanted to remarry but *desired* a very specific type of woman. He *wanted* a woman who would be a devout believer in Jesus, The Christ, and a partner in ministry who was nurturing, motherly, loyal…and…with a fair skin tone.

> ***I know you're thinking…***
> ***"Huh? The color of her skin mattered to a pastor?"***
> ***This will make sense in a minute….***

Yes! *Fair-complected skin* was a *personal desire,* what he *wanted*, and a deciding factor…so he thought. He and his children were fair-complected African Americans. He *wanted* to marry a woman with the same or similar complexion as his children to *cover up* the fact he was a divorced pastor. Apparently, this was a *big deal* and frowned upon in the 1980s.

Well, a year after the divorce, he met his beautiful soon-to-be wife. She was everything he *wanted* and *needed* (before *he* really knew) except…she was *dark brown complected.* She also had a beautiful young dark brown complected daughter. She received salvation at the Bible study session, where they met for the first time. (She was a "Not-So-Obvious Prime Enough" discussed later in Chapter 10.)

God *gave* the pastor a *Godly desire* for the woman. God also *gave* the woman a *Godly desire* for the pastor. Once they *accepted* the *desire* from God by *choice*, they became *Needed Wants / Desires* to each other. The pastor pursued her, and she became increasingly interested in him…

leading to a short thirty-day courtship (which they do not recommend) and marriage.

Today they have been happily married for over twenty-five years, raised their beautiful children to become amazing adults, developed individual and corporate ministries, and are the founders of multiple church locations and counting. They are best friends, lovers, and partners in ministry. Although they weren't each other's *original* type, God knew what they were **destined** to accomplish TOGETHER…**DOMINION!**

They were both given a *Godly desire* from God for what He knew they *needed* and *wanted* long term. Ironically, this included the skin complexion. God is strategic. He used an obviously blended family (due to the different complexions and appearance) to show forth/represent His Glory through the restoration of two divorcees brought together for purpose in ministry and family. Their ministry is highly instrumental in the restoration of marriages and families, pastoring families, preaching to families, and building leaders, to name a few.

God's Will does not align with *our wants* and *personal desires* that are "off" and misconstrued. God's Will aligns with our individual and marital purpose and is revealed through *Godly desire*.

God uses *desire* as the driving force (in the form of passion) to lead us to the *choices* that fulfill our purpose.

> Purpose and destiny are predestined but not automatic. **Choose** it.

Know Your Enemy

What is not from God is a ploy from your adversary Satan to get you "off course," the *course* referred to as God's *perfect Will* for your life. Once *off course*, time is stolen. In addition, beliefs, innate dreams, and goals run the risk of dying. Once "*hope*" is "*deferred,*" the "*heart*" becomes "*sick*" (Proverbs 13:12). Our soul (mind, will, intellect, emotions, and imagination) is negatively impacted with the intent to "*destroy*" our being. This is based on the scripture:

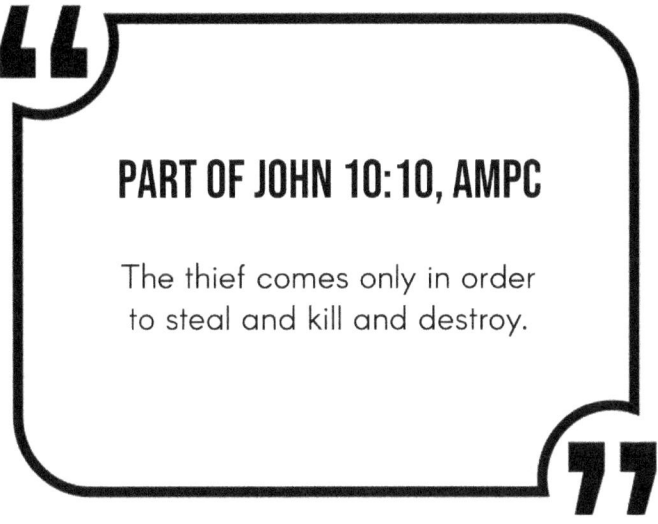

PART OF JOHN 10:10, AMPC

The thief comes only in order to steal and kill and destroy.

There is no guesswork in understanding our true enemy wants to destroy our lives and will use ANYTHING he can, *including* scriptures and the Word of God, to get us to *choose* his ploys for our lives—one crucial decision at a time. *If possible*, Satan (humanity's enemy) will use our thought patterns that ultimately lead to the wrong decisions based on past experiences, cultural and societal influences, worldly/carnal influences, misinterpreted scriptures, improper religious and secular teachings, parental and peer influences, spiritual manipulation, etc. He will attempt to use every part of our soul (mind, will, intellect, emotions, and imagination) if we are not aware of his strategies to get us to *choose* to allow him access.

The scripture referenced above states, "The thief comes…***in order to***…." This means his ploy is NOT an automatic guarantee. **It is simply**

a strategic plan. If it is a plan, it would require our participation *in order to* come to pass. Due to our *free will*, we have the *choice* to intentionally or unintentionally participate in this plan that **does** exist.

Do not be religious-minded and dismiss the fact you have an enemy that hates you and does not take breaks. Knowing your enemy AND his strategies is only half the battle. Using your power *given* through Jesus, The Christ, causes you to triumph over Satan's plans against you.

My Personal Experience

There was a time in my life when I became highly addicted to drugs, including cocaine, molly, cigarettes, and alcohol, during my previous marriage. I also took ecstasy and smoked marijuana, laced cigarettes, and blunts. I always knew this was a ploy to get me *away* from God's Will. Before the substance abuse, I had been saved with a Believer's lifestyle (walking with God) for the past fifteen years. I knew my purpose. I even saw a prophetic vision of my life and the lives God would use me to ultimately reach. I had already started my worldwide music ministry locally and ministered all over Southern California for a few years.

Yet, when tragedy hit, I indulged in several drugs to accompany my mate (at the time) for *his* comfort, in efforts to cover up pain and grief from the recent death of a very close loved one and, most importantly, for the fun! I *chose* to self-medicate in the same way my former partner masked *his* pain—even though that wasn't my *choice* of preference or only "solution." I was addicted to the *fun* we had under the influence and being able to "enjoy" life again…so it seemed…even if it meant putting my goals, dreams, and ministry on hold.

The first time I used cocaine (before the tragedy), it was forced into my system by my ex-mate while I was blindfolded. However, I continued by *choice* once I realized, when under the influence, I did not think about the major issues that were becoming haunting mentally and emotionally. Cocaine served as a *temporary escape* from a lot of **heavy issues** and suspicions that were avoided and never fully confronted, dealt with, or resolved. Even with the abuse and deep relational issues still in existence, drug use provided a way for me to show my "love" towards my ex-partner and be the "fun" me without the mental and emotional hindrances.

Long story short, my "deliverance" (God's ability in me to quit sin) started with first—a *choice*. I knew I couldn't fulfill my purpose if I didn't stop the drug use. I always considered it a temporary fix that would end. I *chose* to STOP. Once the *decision* was **made**, God led me to victory step by step over the course of time. It was a fight…a fight to remain *steadfast*, unwavering, and stern in my *decision* even *after failed* attempts.

I *chose* not to participate in the enemy's plan. I wanted God's purpose for me to be fulfilled like an obsession. I wanted HIM to be my Lord (to lead me). He directed my path towards the ***help*** I needed…***when I needed*** it. It didn't come easy, but I got back on God's plan towards the original destiny, and I was fully delivered from the addictions and spirit of self-sabotage, to name a few.

Back to God's Word…

The scripture continues to further assure us that Jesus has **another plan** for us to experience…and has **made** available the exact *opposite plan* of our enemy's plan for us:

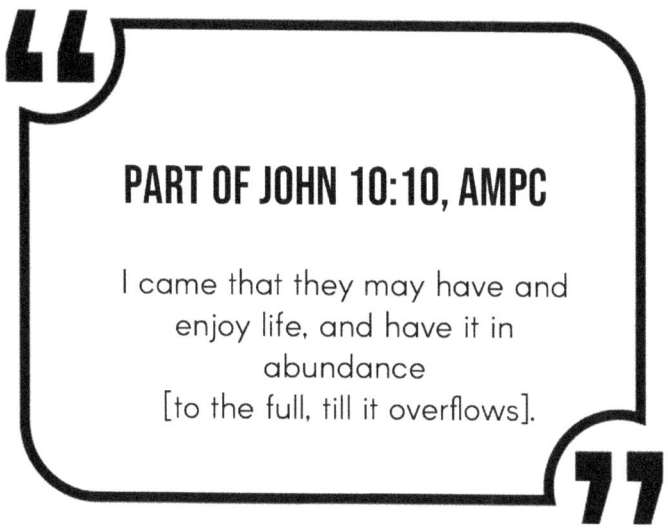

PART OF JOHN 10:10, AMPC

I came that they may have and enjoy life, and have it in abundance
[to the full, till it overflows].

Jesus! This is His plan for us!

But what I also found very interesting is that the *choice* word used in *all* versions of this scripture is **"may"** or **"might"** as it refers to *"have and enjoy life, and have it in abundance"* or *"abundantly."* This means Jesus' plan for us is NOT a guarantee (which is to have and enjoy life in abundance). We "may" or "might" have it. If it is *not* a guarantee, we must have a part to play. It must be CHOSEN.

The "thief" (known as Satan) wants to destroy your life, while Jesus wants to give you life. BOTH *options* require your will to **choose** one or the other.

The ability to *choose* wisely, according to knowledge and discernment, begins with **correctly** interpreting the Word of God. Ideally, the Word of God (Scriptures) should be the premise of all decisions. Understanding the Word is more important than reading it. Understanding the Word also helps us to recognize when the Scriptures are used in the proper context and when it is not to avoid deception. Specifically, the interpretation of **Psalm 37:4** in its proper context will aid our decisions. **It is the compass (for our spirits)** to *destined choices and desires (and our mates who are Desires)*.

What or who do you have an <u>unexplainable desire</u> for...
that is not based merely on your <u>wants</u>?
This is a strong indication of a possible Godly desire.

It is great to know the character traits that qualify someone to accompany our journey and purpose. However, the *safest*, most guaranteed prayer is to pray for God's Will to manifest, and it will—in the form of a *desire* from God Himself. This *"desire"* (mentioned in Psalm 37:4) may or may not (most likely not) look like what (or who) we envisioned, but (he or she) will be exactly what (or who) we *need* and *want* (i.e., a *Needed Want / Desire*). To experience these "desires" and one who is a *Desire* **requires** trust in God, time spent with Him, studying His Word, worship, prayer, belief (in what He reveals), and, most importantly, a personal relationship with the Holy Spirit so you know His voice.

In Conclusion…

As you spend time with God, He will reveal more and more of His Will for you. His Will consists of *His desires* pertaining to the details of His plans for you. The details include *who, what, when, where, and how* the plans will unfold (discussed more in a later chapter, "Timing and Windows…").

Understand the difference between your will and *personal desires* and Gods' Will and *Godly desires*. *Why*? You can ask God for your *personal desires*—but "when you ask, you do not receive, because you ask with wrong motives, that you may spend what you get on your pleasures" (James 4:3, NIV). You *can* go after what *you* want and *your pleasures* and get it, but *it* will not be the Will of God, which is *His plans* for you. God wants us to receive *His desires* for *His good pleasures*. "For it is **God who works in you**, both to **will** and to **work** for **his good pleasure**" (Philippians 2:13).

Be patient to receive *Godly desires* from God. Continuously read and do the Word of God to sharpen your discernment to recognize *God's desires* (versus your *own*). Until the details are revealed in the area of life you are looking forward to experiencing, such as marriage, focus on the details you already know in other areas to avoid obsessing in anticipation for more details. Every detail will be revealed in God's Timing. When you don't *desire* a mate *more* than God is when He will reveal and *give* them to you.

CHAPTER *Six*

THE "COUNTERFEITS": UNDERSTANDING AND IDENTIFYING A "CLOSE-FIT"

"*Counterfeits*" are simply "*Wants*" who are Master Manipulators and masters of perception. Their primary goal is to *appear* as one who is a "*Need*" to get what they *want* **by any means necessary**. They are highly skilled at masking their personalities and character to resemble *Needs* but are far from it. They know how to sway others' perception—in their favor through manipulation—to believe what they want them to believe for self-gain and benefits. The ability to discern a *Counterfeit* requires a clear understanding of those who are *Needs* and the ability to recognize the characteristics of *Needs*. Out of all the other *Options* (such as those who are "*Neithers*" and "*Likes*" described later in Chapter 11), *Counterfeits* are the most deceptive, manipulative, and dangerous type. They are hard to detect without an understanding of how one operates.

Here is an important rule of thumb (especially for those who are *Needs*). If someone with a **majority** of *Want* characteristics is appealing or gravitating to you (aggressively or passively), that person is a *Counterfeit*.

One can also contribute their *own mindset* to *creating Counterfeits* out of *Wants* **and** *Needs* (as well as out of *Likes* [simply crushes] and *Neithers* [those who are unappealing, not considered] when in a desperate state). This is the "Self-Created *Desire Counterfeit*" and is the exception to the deceptive and manipulative type.

Time, generally, is the revealer of truth. However, to avoid timely mistakes, "wasted" time, soul ties, and heartache, this chapter will explain **how to recognize a** *Counterfeit*.

Types of "Counterfeits"

There are several types of *Counterfeits*; they can be male or female. Each type *gravitates* to a specific type of person who can also be **male** or **female**. The (*) indicates the type they *gravitate* to™ can also be a *Want* or a *Need*. All others are most likely a *Want*.

Remember, a *Want* is someone with Worldy characteristics; a *Need* is someone with Godly characteristics. "Single" refers to *unmarried* individuals. (These two people or couples can also be married.)

Here are the various types of *Counterfeits* (but not limited to the following) **AND** the specific types of people they *gravitate* to:

- The Self-Created *Desire Counterfeit* to the *__Admirer/Fantasizer Single__ (Admiring *Need* / Fantasizing *Want*)
- The Hurt-Magnet *Counterfeit* to the *__Hurt Single__
- The Religious *Counterfeit* to the *__God Seeker__
- The Business-Opportunist *Counterfeit* to the *__Ambitious Achiever__
- The Cradle-Robber *Counterfeit* to the **Parental-Attention Seeker**
- The Narcissistic *Counterfeit* to the **Low Self-Worth Single**
- The Refined-Thug *Counterfeit* to the **Not-Good-Enough Single**
- The Pedophile *Counterfeit* to the **Needy Single Parent**

Now let's dive into each type....

The Unique Type: The "Self-Created Desire Counterfeit" to the * "Admirer / Fantasizer Single"

The "Self-Created *Desire Counterfeit*" is unique to the multiple types of *Counterfeits* because they are the **only** ones who are self-created by the "Admirer/Fantasizer Single." This *Counterfeit* can be male or female (or a place, thing, or opportunity) who is viewed as one who is a *Desire* because of one's own admiration, the "close-fit" appeal, and an impatient state that can cause unhealthy covetousness. They are also the **only** Counterfeit who can be a person who is a *Need* or a *Want*.

The most common cause of the Self-Created *Desire Counterfeits* derives from **misplaced admiration**. Just because you *admire* one's level of wisdom, mental or spiritual maturity, their emotional or financial stability, or even the *path* they are on—that does **not** make them necessarily a *Need for you*. A person's brilliance can be admired from afar without them being *God's desired mate for you* (known as a *Needed Want / Desire*).

There are many profound and prevalent admirable people of the opposite sex, such as professionals, leaders, pastors, prophets, evangelists, motivational speakers, homemakers, elders, entertainers, teachers, etc. Whether they are married or *not*, it is not healthy to covet or imagine the possibilities of a romantic relationship on the grounds of admiration.

Many types of relationships can create a Self-Created *Desire Counterfeit* if we are not consciously aware of unhealthy or misplaced admiration. This behavior can also be a spiritual violation within the following relationships: teacher/student, mentor/mentee, pastor/member, etc. This relationship dynamic produces unhealthy behavior when there is no pursuit or clear intentionality, and it creates a one-sided interest from the fantasizing party involved. In addition, the person of interest should not be one of *many* within the same setting (school, congregation, etc.), especially at the same time.

This Admirer/Fantasizer Single (most likely an "Admiring *Need*") is driven by *admiration* and therefore is very accepting of one who *resembles Need* characteristics (or *is* an actual *Need*) although the person is not a *Desire* (who will *always* have a **mutual desire**/interest at some point).

However, due to the high level of admiration and active imagination, the Admirer/Fantasizer Single (most likely a "Fantasizing *Want*") can easily overlook seen and unseen characteristics that categorize one as a *Want, Like, Neither,* or *Counterfeit*. The Fantasizer sees what they *want* to see, simply put, creating a "Self-Created *Desire Counterfeit*."

The "Hurt-Magnet Counterfeit" to the * "Hurt Single"

The "Hurt-Magnet *Counterfeit*" *is one who intentionally seeks or is drawn to hurting people to pursue a romantic relationship. This type of Counterfeit can be male or female (or an "it," such as an opportunity, location, etc.) who is appealing to the *"Hurt Single" (Want or Need) due to their hurting state of being.*

The worst state to make any decision in is the hurting state. People often wonder why "this" or "that" (usually a mate) has not been "discovered" or they haven't received a *desire* for a particular person to pursue (for men) or be pursued by (for women). Many times it is because the person is in a *deeply* hurting state of being, known as the "Hurt Single" (who can be a *Want* or *Need*).

Interestingly enough, on the other hand, God can *reveal* a *Need* to someone hurting, but the progression of that relationship will be *put on hold* until a certain level of healing is reached. This level of healing is generally referred to as "being whole." However, *being whole* is determined by God according to His standard, not man's standards (referred to as "Prime Enough," discussed later in Chapter 9).

No one is exempt from pain. Therefore, when healing is obtained for one set of experiences, *another* healing will be required for *another* painful experience to come. When referring to "being whole," it is the state in which the pain from an experience is no longer *fresh* (among altered or developed characteristics and behaviors—due to pain).

"Fresh" does **not** mean *a recent pain* and has nothing to do with time. *Fresh* refers to the lack of *successful* efforts towards healing. A *fresh* emotional wound can refer to *any* amount of time since the initial painful event—from ten minutes ago to ten-plus years ago and counting. Many *fresh* pains are not always obvious due to the length of time that has passed. If someone is not healed emotionally, the wound is still *fresh*, regardless of the amount of time passed.

The **danger** of making a decision (to begin or progress a relationship) during the *fresh* level of pain is **not** just a possible encounter (or relationship) with a *Counterfeit* who is *drawn* to the hurting person—but the **lens/perception of the hurting person** during this state. He or she will not be able to discern (or recognize) a *Counterfeit* because, again, the *Counterfeit* is a Master Manipulator who studies others' perceptions. He or she (or "it," such as a business opportunity, location, etc.) knows exactly how to *appeal* to one based on the hurt *recognized* in the *"Hurt Single" (usually a "Hurting *Want*"). This *Counterfeit* will offer a "healing solution" that is *wanted*, *needed,* and sometimes *sought* by the hurting person. The *healing solution* will be presented in the form of affection, attention, a listening ear, money, sex, "getaway" vacations, etc.

Can a "Need" Be Hurting?

Generally speaking, according to the definition of a *"Need"* from previous chapters, the answer is "no"—in the sense of having a known *fresh* emotional/relational hurt that has not been dealt with. A *Need* will intentionally seek and successfully reach a level of healing to be considered "whole" in a romantic relationship.

Can New Hurts Arise in a "Need's" Life?

Yes, and most likely will. That is *life* and why it does not disqualify one from being considered a *Need*. However, the new pain will be handled in a mature way, differently than a *Want*. Also, the hurt will not stem from a previous romantic relationship. Instead, if pain is *present* (not *fresh*—due to successful efforts to heal emotional wounds), it will be another form of hurt, such as disappointment, resurfaced pain from the past, or pain involving a non-romantic partner or scenario. So, in essence, a *Need* can also be a "Hurt Single" (also known as a "Hurting *Need*") at certain times in life.

Can a Hurting "Need" Still Become a "Desire" for Another "Need"?

Yes, a hurting *Need* can *still* become a *Desire* for *another Need*. However, it is premature to progress the relationship into a state of engagement or marriage BEFORE the previous hurts from a former relationship(s) are healed. If a *Need* is revealed as a *Desire*, simply place the advancement of the relationship on *hold* until the *appointed time* for a smoother transition into a purposeful marriage. This is one *choice*.

Another *choice* two individuals can make in this situation is to act prematurely and progress the relationship anyway (while hurting from a previous relationship due to an ex-partner(s), family member(s), etc.). But it will be a bumpier ride. This *choice* can cause a divine relationship to be destroyed and disintegrate before it really gets started.

However, if God leads the two to advance the relationship, and one is intentionally dealing with a current hurt, the other person who is a *Desire* from God will have the capacity to aid in any healing process needed, including the deeper hidden hurts.

The best way to avoid the Hurt Magnet *Counterfeit is to wait until you are emotionally healed or stable* **before** *allowing any Option into your personal life.*

The "Religious Counterfeit" to the * "God Seeker"

*The "Religious Counterfeit" is one who uses religion or belief as the main common ground or the bait to hook the * "God Seeker," who can be a Want or Need in some cases. However, this Counterfeit seeks, ideally, the God-seeking Want. The "Religious Counterfeit" is fully aware of the Want's love for God (who is seeking and intrigued by an increase of Godly knowledge) and their inability to discern motives.*

These *Counterfeits* use spiritual and/or religious knowledge to appear as the *ideal mate* for the *Want* or *Need*. Both scenarios differ in outcome due to discernment. *Wants* will not discern this type of *Counterfeit*. A *Need* has the ability to discern this *Counterfeit*.

How Do You Discern a Religious Counterfeit from a TRUE Man or Woman of God?

This *Counterfeit* will use spiritual beliefs and/or religion to *lift **themselves** up*. He or she will refer to themselves as the "ideal mate" because of their spiritual knowledge and maturity. This type overly emphasizes *why* they are the *ideal mate* more than usual in an effort to convince you rather quickly—instead of allowing you to discern or discover their true motives and purpose. This is why they will generally attempt to advance the relationship rather quickly. **Do not be deceived.** They will also lift up Jesus, The Christ, and, in most cases, "god" (the preferred term).

The Religious *Counterfeit* will have the "form of godliness but deny the power thereof" (2 Timothy 3:5, KJV), meaning, they will appear like the devout Christian (follower of Christ) but deny God's power—usually for self-control—and do not live by Christ's morals behind closed doors. They are, in fact, "lukewarm." They are not *all the way in* or *all the way out*. You will not recognize and know this until you get to know them. These behaviors are hidden to **lure** you in emotionally and through your *own desire* to love God, which is why they prefer a committed relationship BEFORE you discover a majority of their characteristics.

The "Business-Opportunist Counterfeit" to the * "Ambitious Achiever"

The "Business-Opportunist *Counterfeit*" *is one who is seeking a business partner or financial benefit. Their motive is to obtain a financially secure lifestyle. This type can also be male or female. They gravitate to* * "Ambitious Achievers" *(who can be* Wants *or* Needs*) who are driven, ambitious, goal oriented, and established or soon-to-be established.*

An example of an obvious Business-Opportunist *Counterfeit* is a "gold digger" (male or female) seeking a professional athlete, entertainer, construction worker, business owner/entrepreneur, etc., or one with a prestigious or criminal career, such as an attorney or drug dealer.

Many *Ambitious Achievers who are *Wants* (known as "Ambitious Achieving *Wants*") may settle for this type of *Counterfeit* knowingly and willingly because most of the *Options* they attract are this type. (*Remember, types attract their similar type.) *Wants*, in general, have less patience and the inability to discern the intentions for the other person's pursuit. They tend to rush the pace and advancement of the relationship due to less mature characteristics and what they are driven by (looks, emotions, sex, image, money, etc.).

*Ambitious Achievers who are *Needs*, on the other hand, are *whole* enough to *pace* the encounter with this type of *Counterfeit* to discern motives and apply patience to wait on God's approval for one who is a *Desire* from Him (*or not*), avoiding wasted time and letdown emotions.

Sometimes this *Counterfeit* is *extremely* obvious (probably the most obvious out of all types mentioned). However, this type is discussed in detail because sometimes they are *not obvious*. Their goal, in order to be *chosen*, is *not* to appear obvious. They will be appealing in many ways, usually through charm, looks, and common interests, to camouflage this motive as best as possible. They can also have hidden motives to accelerate their *own* ambitions and are led by *personal desire* versus the leading of the Holy Spirit. (*God also creates acceleration for **His** plans.)

The world teaches many societies this scenario is common and harmless (whether it refers to an established or aspiring relationship). Although this scenario may *seem* harmless, it is not. It is **harmful** if it is not God's Will for your life.

Again…

- 💍 *Is it possible to live a "good" life?* Yes.

- 💍 *Is it possible to live a "see no evil, hear no evil," "turn the other cheek to sin" life and enjoy the financial benefit and prestige?* Yes.

- 💍 *Will you fulfill your destiny to the fullest?* **No.**

It is important to **choose** purpose (*God's "desire"*) over the seductiveness, engagingness, attractiveness, and charm of the Business-Opportunist *Counterfeit*. Usually in these relationships, if and when the benefits are *secured* without the partner **or** the benefits *cease*, so does the relationship.

The "Cradle-Robber Counterfeit" to the "Parental-Attention Seeker"

The "Cradle-Robber *Counterfeit*" *is one who seeks and gravitates to one who is needy for attention, specifically parental attention, known as the* "Parental-Attention Seeker" *(who is a* Want*). This* Counterfeit *can be male or female and is generally older than the* Want *but not in all cases. They will allure one into a relationship by actually fulfilling a parental role (providing guidance, money, and control).*

These *Counterfeits* are *turned on* by being called "Daddy" or "Mommy" by the *Want*. As flirtatious and innocent as this may seem, it is more appealing to the *Counterfeit* in literal terms. It is subconsciously literal to the *Want* and, therefore, appears natural and flirty (on the surface). This term is also deemed socially acceptable (mainly behind closed doors).

The Parental-Attention Seeker possesses a void of parental guidance, love, attention, and protection from one or both parents.

As a result, it is extremely easy for a "Cradle-Robber *Counterfeit*" to *appeal* to these *Wants'* soul *desires* to satisfy their yearning for parental love and nurturing. (*Soul desires* consist of *personal desires* based on emotions, intellect, will, mental stimulation, *desired* lifestyle, imagination regarding an ideal mate, etc.)

The **danger** is these *Counterfeits* can *seem* like the "perfect match" due to the void that *appears* fulfilled and **mistaken** as God's Will *or* the "on-track life" *or* a healthy relationship (which is an illusion).

The "Narcissistic Counterfeit" to the "Low Self-Worth Single"

The "Narcissistic Counterfeit" is one who is self-centered with a warped definition of "love" and can be male or female. Their primary goal is to be loved and "look good" to others—as a result of being with the complementing Want. Their definition of love is to be treated and loved in a moralistic way as a form of entitlement without reciprocating the same type of love and treatment. Therefore, they intentionally seek "Low Self-Worth Singles."

These *Counterfeits* gravitate to *Wants* with low self-worth because these *Wants* do not love themselves. Most do not possess the ability to discern the selfish, one-sided approach to love that will ultimately become abuse. Those who *can* discern and recognize the selfish, one-sided approach to love *but **still** enter into romantic relationships with Narcissistic Counterfeits* do not love themselves enough to require and only accept better treatment.

These *Counterfeits* seek *this* specific type of *Want*. Why? The Low Self-Worth Singles focus mainly on this type of *Counterfeits'* needs, wants, and *desires*…**without** requiring or expecting the same efforts of loving actions in return. These *Counterfeits* are aware they will be the *center* of the Low Self-Worth Single's life, breeding an unhealthy loyalty. This loyalty to a fault is driven by their continuously increasing efforts to *please* them, investing to no avail, with hopes of it *paying off*—a "harvest" that is **never** experienced. As a result, *delusional expectations* are developed by the *Want* that can never be fully met. Simply put, these *Counterfeits* are **never** satisfied.

Let's get personal…. For someone to be satisfied means you *being* yourself is enough for this person. You will **never** *be enough* or *do enough* for these *Counterfeits*. They infiltrate this belief (into *Wants*) to always keep you doing more. They do not have the understanding and willingness to reciprocate true *Godly love* because this type of love is selfless *versus* self-centered. They are incapable of giving Godly love because they generally do not love themselves or **only** "love" themselves.

Faith is the sustaining element that initially draws this type of *Want* to a Narcissistic *Counterfeit*—because they focus on the **potential** of the

Counterfeit versus the person's current state, character, and treatment towards them presently. Their faith is in the potential they see in the *Counterfeit*.

The Narcissistic *Counterfeit* will remain undetected either temporarily or indefinitely, depending on the *self-worth* of the other person in the relationship. They are temporarily undetected (one month to fifteen-plus years) *until* the *Want* becomes a *Need* (character-wise), and they become **aware** of their true self-worth and **implement** self-love. This *Counterfeit* remains undetected indefinitely *if* the *Want* never discovers their true self-worth, value, and *Godly self-love*. The Narcissistic *Counterfeit* will work overtime, non-stop, subtly, and openly to chip away at their "partner's" self-esteem and self-worth in hopes they never discover their *own* true value, resulting in the *Counterfeit* losing their control and influence.

Side note regarding **self-worth**: *Do not be deceived (tricked). A person can have high self-esteem (derived from the complimenting opinions of others and society's standards that form their opinion of themselves) and low self-worth (derived from their true opinion and view of themselves). This will be reflected by one's behavior and choices (my personal story).*

Lastly, Narcissistic *Counterfeits* are not easily recognized, as their title may suggest. They can appear extremely "loving." At the start of a relationship, they will pretend to support your goals but have a hidden agenda to gain mental and emotional control to tailor and destroy any goals and ambitions that do not meet *their needs* or "prevent" them from being the primary focus (*from their perspective*). They are in constant competition with the other person's success because they view it as threatening to their position. They are not truly supportive. Their support is contingent on their *needs*. They do not see the other person's goals as beneficial for themselves but rather a "threat" due to deeply rooted insecurities. These insecurities will eventually manifest into jealousy. Suppose they are able to see the benefit of another person's goals. In that case, their self-centered complacency will override any *desire* to see and experience the goals accomplished.

The Narcissistic *Counterfeit's* primary method **to stop** the Low Self-Worth Single from purposeful accomplishments is through **mental**,

emotional, and even **spiritual control**. They are usually verbally, mentally, and emotionally abusive, and, in some cases, physically abusive. They will intentionally work at keeping their partner's self-worth low to become or remain the primary focus. Their impact on your self-image (consciously or subconsciously) and emotions makes them extremely dangerous. If and when the *Want* transforms into a *Need*, they will become an Ambitious Achiever; however, the Narcissistic *Counterfeit* will work even harder to stop their ambitious drive or try to tailor it for their *own* benefit. They will attempt to create major limitations and roadblocks to prevent one from reaching their highest potential.

The "Refined-Thug Counterfeit" to the "Not-Good-Enough Single"

The "Refined-Thug Counterfeit" is one who appears to be transformed from a life of immoral behavior but has no knowledge of and/or refused knowledge to truly transform the old mindsets consisting of derogatory behaviors and/or criminal behaviors. This Counterfeit can be male or female, lacking an inner transformation derived from Christian discipleship, meditation on the Word of God, spiritual/leadership accountability, therapy, and counseling/pastoring of the soul. They appear changed from within and, to some degree, are "changed." However, the changes are on the surface (in appearance) and temporary versus permanent. It is a matter of time before these Counterfeits reveal their true colors, both intentionally and unintentionally. They gravitate to "Not-Good-Enough Singles" (who are Wants) who do not believe they are good enough for a partner of a different stature in nature. This Counterfeit strongly attempts to hide their unchanged nature, mentalities, aggressive behaviors, and immoral imperfections from the other person in order to gain acceptance.

Not-Good-Enough Singles are usually familiar with street guys or women due to admiration *or* a shared background *or* family subculture. They do not see themselves as worthy of a different type (also known as a "good guy" or "good girl," one *without* a street background or one who's more Godly in character). As a result, they will allow this type into their lives as long as he or she *appears* "reformed."

These couples will appear as a "perfect match" because their *street side* (or *hood side*) will be what they both have in common, which eradicates any potential judgment of each other for flaws or behaviors that are considered "ghetto" (in reference to subcultural expressions, behaviors, and mentalities—not ethnicity).

Refined-Thug *Counterfeits* may also gravitate to the Not-Good-Enough Singles who *do not* have a street background in common and are attracted to each other due to the "opposites attract" syndrome (opposite backgrounds, interests, nature, etc.).

The common denominator for all of these *Wants* is their personal belief of themselves: the unworthiness of a certain type of mate. This belief causes them to accept a person that is not a *Need* based on the "Representative" version of the person first presented (generally within the first six to twelve months). They may also accept the person prematurely (*if the Counterfeit is a Need in the making*).

Some of these *Counterfeits* will also attend church services (including online), both regularly or sporadically. Church attendance *does not* necessarily imply true transformation and discipleship.

These *Counterfeits'* characteristics do not apply to *all* men and women with street backgrounds who have reformed their lifestyles. This definition applies to those who attempt to *appear* "reformed" but, in fact, are not (or *yet*…in some cases). They know they are not *reformed* and are *"faking it until they make it,"* as some would say, but do not disclose this knowledge of self (*through honesty and transparency*) to the other person / *Want*. Underneath the fraudster, they have abusive tendencies—physically, emotionally, financially, and/or verbally. They also may engage in criminal behavior.

The Refined-Thug *Counterfeit"* may also attempt to strongly or subtly persuade you to engage in or join them in criminal behavior.

Those who are *Needs* have the ability to discern this type of *Counterfeit*; therefore, avoid these relationships on the basis of being spiritually **unequally** yoked (*which also denotes mentally, emotionally, **ethically**, and **morally**—unequally yoked*), to say the least, or due to a different preference but not because of their *street* background, per se.

The "Pedophile Counterfeit" to the "Needy Single Parent"

The "Pedophile Counterfeit" purposely seeks and gravitates to the needy single mother or single father, also known as the "Needy Single Parent" (who is a Want). This Counterfeit is driven by a lustful spirit that seeks the fulfillment of perversion at any cost, specifically the innocence of children.

Needy parents (both single and married) will usually be blinded to the behaviors and actions of this type of Counterfeit *(which is directly or indirectly towards their child or children)* **due to** his or her focus that is on their *own wants and needs* as well as the Counterfeit's *wants and needs*.

The Pedophile Counterfeit is highly aware that the Needy Single Parent will put their *own needs* before the well-being of their child (or any minors in their care) to receive what they *perceive* as "love" from the Counterfeit or to meet a *need*. As a result, these Counterfeits will invest time into this relationship to receive *immediate* or *future* access to children to lust over them, molest them physically or mentally (without touch), or groom them emotionally (to fulfill *lustful desires*).

Warning Regarding ALL Counterfeits for Those with Kids

Any type of Counterfeit can be abusive towards your child (or children) verbally, mentally, emotionally, or physically. Remember, the Counterfeit is not the person God desires for you to be with. This is why it is important to know who you truly are and not be desperate for a relationship. In addition, if the Counterfeit has a child (or children), the way they treat *them*—if moralistically—is not always an indication of how they will treat *other* children (including those you have with them).

Can Someone Be More Than One Type of Counterfeit?

Absolutely! A Counterfeit is a Counterfeit. They have a spiritual agenda to derail God's plans for one's life (knowingly or unknowingly). They will use any and all methods possible to get the person they *want* in order to project and acquire what they *personally desire*.

*Combined *Counterfeit* characteristics reflect one's agenda (method)/goal (objective).

There are numerous combinations in which one can possess characteristics of more than one type of *Counterfeit*. Other combinations are unlikely to be combined. Here are only a few examples of *likely* and *unlikely combinations*.

Examples of Combined Counterfeit Characteristics

The **Religious / Pedophile** *Counterfeit* is one who has pedophile characteristics that can be overlooked due to the religious/spiritual persona. This type will use religion to gain trust from both parent and child and eventually gain control to act out their perverted ambitions.

The **Cradle-Robber / Pedophile** *Counterfeit* will capitalize off the neediness of a parent to gain trust from both parent and child, and eventually gain *control* to act out their perverted ambitions. They will have a similar goal as the example above (to gain access to children for perverted reasons) but will gain access to the *Want's* heart through a different method. They will use the *Want's need* for parental guidance to *gain access* into their life to act out perverted ambitions with the children of the *Want*.

The **Refined-Thug / Narcissistic** *Counterfeit* is one who is chosen for all the *wrong* reasons, such as a street persona or street background (whether shared in common or not) yet lacks the Godly characteristics of a *Need*. They will try to appear ethical to gain a person's interest (even though they are not). He or she is only interested in being loved moralistically and receiving *Godly love* without being held accountable to reciprocate *Godly love* to the other person (which is their goal).

The **Refined-Thug / Business-Opportunist** *Counterfeit* will gain the interest of the *Want* through their appealing street persona/background (whether shared in common or not) and try to appear ethical (even though they are not). However, their objective is to gain access to the lifestyle and current or future finances one can provide versus a *God-given* purpose. They will have an agenda similar to the example described above—but a different goal.

Example of an Unlikely Combination of Counterfeit Characteristics

The *Narcissistic / Business-Opportunist Counterfeit:* These two types of *Counterfeits* are similar with two different focal points. The *main* goal of the Narcissist *Counterfeit* is to be loved and the center of one's world, and they will *eventually* try to stop any ambition they think "prevents" their self-centered agenda. The Business-Opportunist *Counterfeit's* main goal is to obtain a specific lifestyle; therefore, they will *never* stop any ambition.

Both types usually have seemingly harmless motives, which is why they are undetectable *Counterfeits*. *If this unlikely combination exists, one set of characteristics will be more prevalent than the other. They may only want you to succeed at helping *them* while taking advantage of you and discouraging you from your personal goals. Nevertheless, neither type will be a person who's a *Desire* given by God.

In time, these types of *Counterfeit* characteristics can change. Remember, timing is **inclusive** (and a HUGE part) of God's Will/plans.

However, **always base your judgment and decisions on the person's characteristics presented before you at the PRESENT TIME.**

"Counterfeits" Versus "Neithers": Understanding the Difference

It is important to understand and remember the difference between "*Counterfeits*" and "*Neithers*" (discussed in detail later in Chapter 11).

"*Neithers*" are those who you do not *like, want,* or *need,* and this is obvious "out the gate." *Counterfeits* are NOT obvious and, in fact, seem like the exact opposite of their descriptions. They appear to be *nothing* like the titles used to describe each type. If they did, they would *instantly* be categorized as *Neithers* and not considered an *option*. Instead, they will *appear* to be the "*perfect match*" beyond the "honeymoon" and *Representative Phase* of a relationship. (*The "Representative Phase" is generally the first few months to two years of a relationship in which each person is revealing their most impressive side of their personality, known as the "Representative.")

The main point to remember is *Counterfeits* are *highly* appealing (specifically to those who are *Wants*)!

The *Good News* is *Counterfeits* and *Neithers* can be discerned by your spirit using the Word of God!

> ## HEBREWS 4:12, KJV
>
> For the Word of God is quick, and powerful, and sharper than any two-edged sword, piercing even to the dividing asunder of soul and spirit, and of the joints and marrow, and is a discerner of the thoughts and intents of the heart.

Choosing to be with a *Neither*—someone you're not *really* interested in—is a matter of desperation and deception. **Not** choosing a *Counterfeit* can be *way* trickier. But remember, discerning and avoiding a *Counterfeit* is more than preventing a potential divorce; it can also be a matter of life or death. Men and women are losing their lives by getting with or marrying the wrong person. This includes getting into a relationship—on any level—with someone who is a *Counterfeit* or *Neither*.

The Word of God is your tool…your lifeline…to help you *choose* the right mate based on *Godly wisdom*. **Use it**.

How to Discern the "Counterfeit"

#1: Use God's Word

God and His Word are one. His Word is inclusive of, but not limited to, the written Holy Scriptures. God can give you a *specific* WORD; however, it will be confirmed by the Holy Scriptures. In addition, His Word is the only discerner of "the intentions of the heart." If you *stick to,* study, and follow **God's ways**, the intentions of the person's heart (including yours) **will** be revealed in time. Intentions can be **revealed** through a sermon, a movie, a blog, a commercial, a social media post, nature, while reading God's Word, in a dream, through Godly council, while driving or praying, etc. God has many ways in which He communicates. They can even be revealed during conversations and chats (directly or indirectly). Be open-minded to receive His guidance, however it may come.

The Word of God will reveal what derives from your soul and what derives from your spirit. The Word of God will also reveal what derives from another person's soul and what derives from another person's spirit. *How do you know the difference?* What derives from a person's spirit will mirror the Word of God. Anything contrary to the Word of God derives from the soul. If you put God's Word first, the intentions of a person's heart will be revealed and will be for you or against you, simply put.

#2: Examine the Fruit / Results of the Relationship

In all relationships, the person will lead you closer to God or away from God. This reveals if the person is led by the Holy Spirit or their soul (personal motives, agendas, fleshly appetites, etc.). If they lead you closer to God, they are led by the Holy Spirit and most likely not a *Counterfeit*. (But keep in mind, "desire," timing, and free will play a major part in the establishment of a romantic relationship.) If they lead you away from God, they are a *Counterfeit*. (Religious *Counterfeits* appear to lead you closer to God initially—but will eventually lead you away from God.)

(More ways to discern a *Counterfeit* are in the workbook and webcourse for this book, using an in-depth, personalized process to know *who's who* and *what's what*.)

#3: Work on Yourself

Counterfeits are the most deceptive *type* of person who is a *Want*, and they generally *gravitate* to *other Wants* and seem like the "ideal mate" on the surface. Therefore, the best way to *avoid* such "wolves in sheep's clothing" is to work on **yourself** and not be a *Want* but become a person who is a *Need*. *Wants* attract *Wants*, and *Needs* attract *Needs*.

More Critical Insight Regarding "Counterfeits"

If one has already *chosen* a *Counterfeit* and is currently in a relationship, the relationship will most likely end **once** the person who is a *Want* becomes a *Need*. Deception becomes irradiated and eradicated, and *self-love* (the **God** *in self*) begins to drive all decisions moving forward with the help of the Holy Spirit.

There are exceptions in which the *Need* (who was previously a *Want* in the relationship) will return to a past relationship. So, it does happen (EXCEPT when certain spiritual violations and laws have been broken by a Pedophile *Counterfeit*, for example). First, the relationship MUST "die," meaning the relationship must end (for an allotted time). Meanwhile, the *Counterfeit* has the opportunity to *become* a *Need*—or not. Suppose the *Counterfeit* becomes a *Need* within the allotted *window* of time. In that case, it is *possible* they can get back together through a *God-given desire*… NOW as *Desires* for each other.

Counterfeits are those whose motives are not right or pure. The reason a *Counterfeit* can *become* a *Need* is because it is *possible* for motives to *change* and Godly character to develop. This is a rare process within the same relationship. They usually change and start a new relationship.

Remember, unless you *choose* not to grow and be "arrested" developmentally by, again, *choosing* not to learn, YOU WILL CHANGE. *Counterfeits* generally do not. They have consented to an unseen assignment to *derail* your destiny and keep you off the course of God's Will both intentionally and unintentionally. The main point is that a *Counterfeit* is not one *given* by God as a person who is a *Desire* from Him, regardless of how *ideal* they seem.

Sometimes clear discernment takes patience. Get to know a person without emotion, and time will reveal true intentions…IF you listen to what the person is saying. Jesus called out the Pharisees *after* they spoke, which revealed their heart. A reference to this occurrence is Matthew 12:22–37. Jesus said,

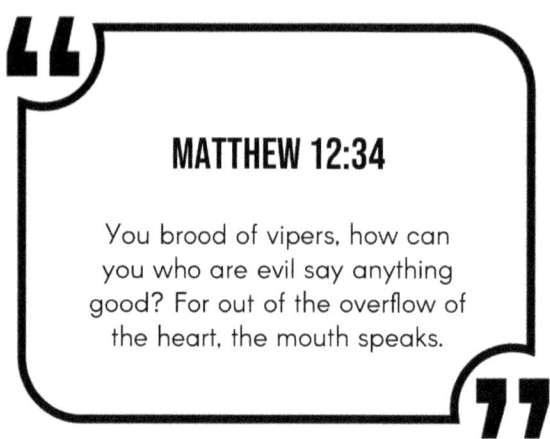

MATTHEW 12:34

You brood of vipers, how can you who are evil say anything good? For out of the overflow of the heart, the mouth speaks.

The intentions of a person's heart will eventually be verbally expressed and exposed. Apply patience, guard and control your emotions, and simply LISTEN (as you observe actions).

The Progression of Influential Voices That Lead to Choosing Counterfeits

When in the position, as an unmarried person, to seek God's Will for a spouse and *choose* someone, be careful of other *voices*. "Voices" pertain to outside influences that seek to sway you in the direction of *their* opinions regarding a mate for you—using their position (or the lack thereof) in your life. The root to all advice, "wisdom," and opinions (which is sometimes referred to as "wisdom") is **NOT** always the Holy Spirit…but can *also* derive from a **spirit** of manipulation, control, bitterness, and jealousy **or** ignorance (a lack of knowledge, information, or understanding).

(Read James 3:14–17 to understand God's Word regarding the **two *sources*** of "wisdom" and the descriptions of each type: ***pure wisdom*** [without partiality and hypocrisy, peaceable, etc.] vs. ***demonic wisdom*** [jealousy, selfish, sensual, etc.].)

It is imperative to guard your ears and heart from being *seeded* with personal opinions, especially from those with a strong influence on your life. There is nothing wrong with *opinions* with seemingly *good* intentions. Just know God will not reveal your mate to *you* for the first time through another person. He may give you a *confirmation* through others regarding your mate. But others will not be used to *reveal* anything the Holy Spirit has not first revealed to you directly (whether you realized and acknowledged or not, it was the Holy Spirit's/God's doing).

The opinions of others can be used unintentionally to derail you from the Word of God and His Will. **It is imperative to your future that you hear from the Holy Spirit personally.**

Once you hear from the Holy Spirit, guard what HE reveals…*meaning*, do NOT tell anyone the Holy Spirit does not unction you to reveal this information to. *Their* personal opinions can be shared with you to *try* to sway you in the direction of *their choice* for you and who they *think* is "right" for you. No one is *more* right than the Holy Spirit. Stick to *your* knowing from the Holy Spirit. **This is the essence of "following your spirit" as it is being led by the Holy Spirit.** He will guide your *choices*, including to the *right* person and away from the *wrong* one.

If a relationship is not right, you WILL know. It will not feel right in your spirit (which is different from your soul, which houses your *preferences, opinions, likes, curiosities, etc.*).

The flip side of this is, if it *does* feel right in your spirit (again, which is different from your soul), it is because it *is*…and this is a strong indication of one who is a *God-given Desire*. **Do not** allow the opinions of others (*whether stated directly or indirectly against your discovery*) to influence you to go against what the Holy Spirit *has* revealed or *is* revealing. In addition, be aware of the various strategies of the enemy, Satan. He is very capable (according to *what* and *who* you set your *secret desires, curiosities, and affections* on) of deceiving you into thinking (and, in some cases, *believing*) that someone is a mate and revealed by God that is not. He can cause *you* to misinterpret a WORD from God, give a false dream (you *think* is from God), or even reveal a face while praying (**all based on** your *own* curiosities). These are some of the ways the enemy can deceive you to willingly *choose* a *Counterfeit*.

The CLEAR GIVEAWAY to knowing if an *Option* is from the enemy (Satan) **or** God is the presence of **CONFUSION and DOUBT** *or* **PEACE** (clear and tangible *peace*) at the ***start*** of a decision. (*Once a certain amount of time passes, one can begin to convince themselves* that wrong is "right" **and/or** right is "wrong.")

When God speaks, it will NOT leave a residue of confusion, doubt, and a lack of peace. **Peace settles a matter.** There is no wavering in the decision or conviction driven by HIM (the Holy Spirit) or double-mindedness.

If you *believe* you heard from God yet are NOT settled in a matter, you have either misinterpreted His Word (to mean what you *want* it to mean) and/or the enemy, Satan, has deceived you into believing one of his methods of deception was from God. These methods of deception *include* the influential voices of one (or more) you have a *soul tie* to (*knowingly or unknowingly*), convincing you to detour from or delay the Will of God. Again, the enemy can use another person you **trust** to try to **convince** you to *choose* a *Counterfeit* (*"suggesting" versus "convincing" are different*). Again, I can't reiterate this enough: The enemy **can** show you a face, speak during prayer, or give you a dream, to list a few. The enemy **can** even speak through a sermon (*deep, I know*), a pastor, a false prophet, a deceptive speaker, or a stranger (including some online "teachers"). These are the most common methods of deception. The enemy can only use thoughts to *try* to deceive you—in an attempt to impact your soul. He does NOT have access to your spirit. The thoughts will be seemingly pleasant.

The objective of these deceptive methods is to throw off your judgment and cause *you* to willingly *make* decisions outside of the Will of God. *Why*? Because the person who is a *Desire* that God motivates you to *choose* and advance *that* relationship to marriage according to HIS timing is EXTREMELY POWERFUL! The marriage will accomplish DOMINION *out the gate* and be used for the Kingdom of God and win souls out of darkness and into the Body of Christ.

The objective of relationships with *Counterfeits* is *far* greater than your personal happiness affected. If entertained and advanced to marriage, it impacts what God originally planned for you to accomplish through *HIS Desire* for you in a covenant marriage of HIS *choice* with a preordained purpose.

The good news is, God can *still* fulfill His purpose through you in a different way. The same destiny will be reached from a different path.

For those divorced, God will use the *Godly wisdom* and experience gained to *also* advance HIS Kingdom—if you love HIM. (Romans 8:28)

Do **not** believe what some may teach…that "you **have to** experience the *bad* to learn and appreciate the *good*." This is simply not true. However, when this is the outcome of life experiences, it is because of God's Mercy, Grace, and His Word that promises us who love God that "…all things work together for *good* to those who love God, to those who are called according to His purpose" (Romans 8:28, NKJV). Many divine couples did not, as single individuals, experience several bad/abusive relationships before marriage yet have the Godly wisdom of those who did—because the "Holy Spirit teaches ALL things" (John 14:26).

The Correlation Between "Wants" and "Counterfeits"

To comprehend the next section, it is essential to understand the correlation between those who are *Wants* and *Counterfeits*.

Wants are not necessarily *Counterfeits* indefinitely, although *Counterfeits* are *Wants* (except for some Self-Created *Desire Counterfeits*). Remember, *Wants* are those who demonstrate Worldly characteristics that drive immature decisions, influencing the *choice*-making process. They **can** (*and some will*) become *Needs* **once** they **transform** their ways through the renewing of their minds (using the Word of God), resulting in more mature *choices*/decisions. A *Want* can be a future spouse; however, this person is not *nearly* ready until they resemble Christ more and become a *Need*. They also can have a *desire* to fulfill the Will of God but simply don't know how yet.

Wants are other singles (*although they can also be married*) and can be friends, associates, etc. and even potential mates after transformation. They are at a phase in life were spiritual maturity and adapting to God's ways needs to develop. When male or female *Wants* pursue another or are in a relationship (*prematurely before they resemble Christ-like characteristics*), they become a *Counterfeit*.

Counterfeits, on the other hand, are either *in* or *seeking* a relationship or marriage **and** they attempt to **APPEAR** as *Needs* in a deceptive manner to be considered. They are *Wants* because their primary purpose for the relationship is NOT fulfilling the Will of God (the opposite characteristics and objective of Jesus, The Christ). It is to gain personal satisfaction through a personal agenda **by any means necessary**. This behavior resembles the mindset, motives, and characteristics of a *Want* which are considered *Worldly*. They only *appear* as those who are *Needs*. However, *Wants* appear as *Wants* and it is apparent.

Counterfeits are *also* at a phase in life where spiritual maturity and adapting to God's ways needs to develop.

(The exception to this behavior is the Self-Created *Desire Counterfeit*.)

The Strategic Pattern of Options: How OPTIONS Generally Present Themselves

When God is getting ready to *give you* one who is His *Desire* for your heart, *Options* tend to present themselves in the following strategic pattern/order:

*Other Option… Desire… *Other Option…

This is the equivalent to:

*Other Option: **"Soul desire"** (*Want, Like, Counterfeit, Need*)**…then**

Desire: **"Godly desire"** (*Desire*)**…then**

*Other Option: **"Soul desire"** (*Want, Like, Counterfeit, Need*)**…**

"*Other Option*" refers to **any** *other* person who is **NOT** the one who is the *Desire* **from** God. These **Other Options* present themselves (intentionally or unintentionally) in an **order** to cause you to second-guess God's *choice / Desire* for your life. This pattern is presented BEFORE marriage. It does not refer to AFTER marriage as its primary strategic goal is to get you off course, which is the actual Will of God regarding marriage.

Specifically, the purpose of this strategic pattern is to get *you* to choose the *Want, Like, Need,* or *Counterfeit* that is presented BEFORE or AFTER the **reveal** or **acceptance** of the one who is the *Desire*.

Understanding the First and Second *Other Option: The *"Soul Desire"*

The first and second **Other Options* are "soul desires" (*Wants, Likes, Counterfeits, Needs*) who present themselves before and after the reveal or **acceptance** of the person who is the *Desire*.

Now that you are aware of this strategy of your enemy according to knowledge, do not be deceived. Recognize this strongly appealing second **Other Option* in the pattern…the final *soul desire / *Other Option* (usually a person who is a *Want*). This strategy can consist of the reoccurrence of the same person who is a *soul desire* (*Want, Like, Counterfeit,* or *Need*) presented before the *Desire* **or** an entirely new person. Whether the person is familiar or new, the second **Other Option* is the *Counterfeit*. They will have a much **stronger** appeal.

For example, you meet *Option* A. Next, you meet and accept the one who is a *Desire*, and then you meet *Option* B. Although *Option* A and B are *Counterfeits*, *Option* B is the second **Other Option / Counterfeit* with a stronger appeal to derail you from marrying the *Desire*. Or *Option* A resurfaces and tries harder.

If, in fact, you cease interest in the *Desire*; entertain the first, second, or *any* **Other Option*; and then realize the **Other Option* is a *Counterfeit*, you may *try* to return to the same one who is the *Desire*. Entertaining this pattern is a risk because the *window of opportunity* to advance the relationship with the same *Desire* may close.

This pattern only occurs surrounding the *Desire*. You may encounter one *soul desire* or multiple in a row—until you encounter a *Godly desire* again.

If you are in a relationship with the one who is a *Desire* and you *cheat* with the **Other Option* (emotionally or physically), you may also lose the *Desire*.

Simply understand, there will always be an *Other Option before and after* meeting the one who is the *Desire* from God.

The Detrimental Impact of Soul Ties

The **#1 *blinder*** to identifying *Counterfeits* are "soul ties." Unhealthy *soul ties* blind you from recognizing an *Option* as a *Counterfeit* and *choosing* the one who is a *Need given* by God.

Therefore, the ultimate goal of *soul desires* (*as *Other Options*) is to create a *soul tie*—so you are continuously lured in through seduction by your *own* will and lust.

Choosing the first *soul desire* (*before the Godly desire is revealed*) can **prevent** you from **recognizing** and **accepting** the *Need* as the *Desire* due to the *soul tie*. Choosing the second *soul desire* (*after accepting the Godly desire*) creates a **major detour** to the plans of God for your life.

If you are unable to *break away (and sever the soul tie)* during the allotted window of time, this *choice* can rob you of time and your original path towards destiny. You may still experience a "good life," an average life…even a life considered "wholesome." However…

> **…you will never experience the fullness of what God intended your life to be on Earth while with the wrong person.**

In Conclusion...

Understanding *Counterfeits* and how to recognize a *Counterfeit*, especially the most common types, will sharpen your discernment to avoid costly *choices*. *Counterfeits* are only as strong as allowed and can only be affective by *choice*. One must use their *own* will to stop the move of God and get out of line with God's Will.

Counterfeits are designed and sent on assignment (*unknowingly*) by your enemy, Satan, to waste your precious time and cause emotional pain that can paralyze progress, sometimes temporarily and sometimes permanently—also by *choice*. Choosing *Counterfeits* can cost you years of your life. In more severe cases, this decision can **cost you your *life*.**

If you are attracting *Counterfeits* often, it is an indication to *really* examine yourself (such as your character, healing, motives, relationship and time spent with God, and voids in your life). It is time to take a break from romantic relationships and *allow* God to complete His perfect work in you to make you *whole*. As a result, you will more easily discern *Counterfeits*.

A safeguard (and indication you are ready to explore *Options* safely) is to be driven by purpose and Godly character based on what you **see** and **not** what *you* want it to be, which, in essence, creates a false image of a person, becoming image-driven versus purpose-driven.

You are now **empowered** to *discern* a "Close-Fit *Counterfeit*" (*versus* a person who is a true *Desire*) and to *choose wisely*, according to knowledge, **who to allow into your life** and on what level, to what degree, and for what purpose.

CHAPTER *Seven*

PREPARATION & PURSUIT

Preparation and *pursuit* as they pertain to marriage and *Options* can be viewed from two *entirely* different perspectives: the **world's process and standards** and **God's process and order**.

Preparation for Marriage

The World's Perspective of Preparation

The world has a system. Within this system are *processes and standards* that society deems "fit," acceptable, and applicable to humanity. Simply put, the world's systems teach people that ***preparation*** for marriage is **less important** than one "following their heart" and emotions to be in a relationship with the one they intend to marry.

This process is a dangerous way of life because our hearts and emotions can be manipulated, wicked, wounded, and misleading. It teaches us to "test the waters," which consists of premature behaviors that lead to *soul ties*, spiritual blindness, confusion, heartbreaks, and a lack of boundaries. Examples of such premature behaviors (*mistaken* as "preparation") are *living together before marriage, sex before marriage, joint bank accounts before marriage, children before marriage*…you get the point, and the list goes on. This mindset is where the "standard" comes into play. The person either "measures up" to the *standards* for what we *want* or *need*—or not. Based on the knowledge and experiences obtained through these actions, determinations are made on whether to move forward to marriage. None of these experiences are God's way of preparing one for marriage or revealing His Will. As a society, these are actions we *choose* according to knowledge based on what we have been taught or witnessed to represent "preparation."

These standards and tests oppose faith because they *require* experiences to determine what *should be* obtained by faith, the leading of the Holy Spirit, and/or a WORD from God.

God's Way for Preparation™

God's way of preparing for marriage consists of a process and order as well as various phases. Although men and women must prepare for marriage in phases, the *dynamics* of these phases shift according to gender.

Phase One: Acknowledgment

Phase One of preparation, which applies to males and females, is simply *acknowledgment*…acknowledging one's *desire* to be married.

This seems like a "given" versus a phase, but believe it or not, many people delay the preparation process by being in denial. They convince themselves they don't want to be married "*right now*" or are "*not thinking about marriage*" when, in actuality, they are not being honest with themselves. This lack of self-honesty could be due to the notion that desiring marriage is a "*desperate,*" frowned-upon state of mind or they "*don't need the opposite sex.*"

Phase Two: "Sleeping Adam" & "Reforming Eve" Preparation

Phase Two is solely preparation for males and females. This process is the "Sleeping Adam" and "Reforming Eve" phase in which God cultivates and builds character to sustain the family dynamics and legacy. It is crucial to allow God to complete this process. This requires complete transparency with God and a mentor for accountability in all areas and thought processes. If not, there will be "dormant flaws" that can cause one to stumble and, in some cases, lose all they have built.

For example, a person has a *lustful desire* for a particular type of attention (outside of their mate's attention). Suppose instructions to rectify this *lustful desire* are not obtained and practiced (during the preparation phase). In that case, this *dormant flaw* (although it appears *hidden*) will resurface after marriage; it can lead to extra-marital affairs (both physically or emotionally). If a person has a gambling obsession or drug addiction that appears *controlled* (another misused word for "*hidden*") before marriage, it will resurface and increase after marriage.

God has a plan and strategy to work on your character and integrity. During Phase Two, character will be built to gird up, sustain, and maintain family structure, dynasties, and empires to achieve DOMINION. This is God's destiny for your life.

For **men**, while "Adam is asleep," God will *purge* them of toxic behaviors, relationships, and *ungodly desires* while *cultivating* them to be a Godly husband in conduct, habits, character, nature, and stature to resemble Jesus.

For **women**, while "Eve is reforming," God is doing a similar work and will *purge* them of toxic behaviors, relationships, and *ungodly desires* while *reforming* them to be a Godly wife in conduct, habits, character, nature, and stature to resemble Jesus.

If the process is completed, he or she will not be "perfect" but worthy of the next phase.

Phase Three: The "Awakened Adam" Pursuit (Men)

The male pursuit is a fascination of mine.... It consists of natural instincts, intuition for a set of *wants* and *needs*, and, ideally, an unction from God (whether God is recognized and credited or not).

During Phase Three, the **"Awakened Adam" has the ability to see who God has made for him as a companion, helpmate, lover, and friend.** There is an *innate desire* for the woman/wife God has **created, formed, revealed, and prepared** for him as a lifelong mate. This *desire* will align with God's "desire"/Will. It is not questionable because it came from God as a result of His process while the male was "sleeping." During this phase, the male will begin his pursuit of the female *Need* whom God has revealed and *given* him a "desire" for—upon awakening (Genesis 2:21–22). *He is the Pursuer.*

Women, if you know who God has revealed to you as a *Need*/mate (and you have not used your words against it) and he can't *see* you yet, he has not awakened. Any decision during his time of *sleep* is a *sleepwalking decision*. And know that he may or may not wake up AFTER a *sleepwalking decision* due to deception or until it's too late and you've moved on. (I will discuss this more in Chapter 12. KEEP reading!)

Phase Three: The "Reformed Eve" Pursued (Women)

Women will have a similar experience as the "Awakened Adam" in the sense that their *desire* for a specific man/husband will align with God's "desire"/Will. This innate *Godly desire* will be for a male *Need* who possesses the characteristics of a man of God **and** does **not** deny God's power...known as the "Awakened Adam." She will recognize him AFTER she is *reformed* in preparation to be a Godly wife/*Need* herself. She is the "Reformed Eve."

During Phase Three, the **Reformed Eve will know who God created her from and for.... In other words, she, *too*, will recognize her husband before or while being pursued.** *She is the Pursuee (the one pursued),* **never** *the Pursuer.* (This does not mean she does not express mutual interest. She's simply not aggressively pursuing nor using lustful seduction, subtly or overtly.)

The Reformed Eve has a posture to **ask** God who her husband is, **hear** HIS voice, and **accept** the answer HE gives. Her question will derive from an *open heart* for God's Will, *not* her own opinions, will, lustful seduction, and *soul desires*. Her **spirit will respond**, not her soul (which is the mind, will, emotions, imagination, and intellect), which can be misled. Next, her **soul's response will *follow***, with **intelligent thought** regarding **suitability and purpose**, an array of **emotions**, and a **willingness** to obey God's instructions. This woman *chooses* the male while still in preparation for marriage. This order is the stage in which Eve saw Adam and knew who he was to her (*"for God brought her to him..."* Genesis 2:22) but had not yet slept together for sexual intimacy. God brought Eve to Adam; then they were both complete (Genesis 2:22–23) and consummated their union.

According to the laws of the land within our society, marriage begins once:

1. a marriage license is obtained;

2. an ordained minister, person of authority with legal authorization, or marriage officiant (religious or civil), etc., conducts the ceremony;

3. vows are exchanged; and

4. it is witnessed by a third party.

Once married, according to these requirements, the preparation has ended, and husbandly/wifely duties are *expected* and desired to be performed regularly.

Do NOT Interrupt or Interfere with God's Process

Men, do **not** try to *create, form,* or *change* "Eve" (women during their re-formation, purging, and preparation phase). Women, do **not** try to *create, form,* or *change* "Sleeping Adam" (men during their development for "husbandhood," purging, and preparation phase). Adam was asleep while Eve was formed, and he was in preparation for a covenant with a wife. They did not interact while she was being formed. (In the case of women today, they are *re-formed*.) Adam was being prepared to embrace Eve upon awakening. He had nothing to do with her process of being formed as a wife, and she had nothing to do with his process of becoming a husband. You are better off being "blind" to each other's individual process during this phase.

Allow God to complete the work He started and form two *whole* individuals. When two individuals destined to be together *try* to help God by correcting each other's flaws prematurely, it changes the dynamics of the relationship from *mates in preparation* to a *mentor/mentee* relationship. It can also lead to *parent/child* or *teacher/student* relationships. These are all abnormal types of relationships when romance is involved; the power dynamic can be harmful. These types of relationships don't work in most marriages (although rare exceptions exist).

Disrupting God's process and order also leads to *doubt* in the one who is a *God-given Desire* when one hinders, **in any way**, the Holy Spirit from completing His work (within the other). *The most common hindrance is sexual intimacy (groping, grinding, French kissing, intercourse, etc.). People generally* **replace** *the leading of the Holy Spirit with emotions and their fleshly desires. The* **next** *most common hindrance are your* **own** *words. Be mindful of your words and do not speak against yourself, your future, or the marriage you desire. Your words have power. (Proverbs 18:21)*

Pursuit: Understanding PURSUIT Beyond the Surface

<u>Men Pursue, Women Choose</u>

Usually when a man pursues, he is tunnel-focused on the "Reformed Eve" / *Need* he recognizes and has an *unexplainable desire* for.

Women are not naturally focused on pursuing. (It is an act that is now culturally influenced.) However, they can be pursued by more than one male, giving her *options*. This is why she is in the position to *choose*.

Men must compete with other Pursuers. The one who aligns with God's Will (timing, windows, purpose, character, and lifestyle) is chosen by the woman—ideally from a *Godly desire* or WORD from God.

If the man is NOT pursuing, he is not putting himself in a position to be *chosen* (by the type of woman who does not chase and/or is led by the Holy Spirit). Only a woman who *does* pursue or chase will *choose* a man who is NOT pursuing.

Here is the *common mistake*: If a woman **pursues** (which is *not* the same as showing *interest*), the man is *now* in the position to *choose*. In addition, it is a *turnoff* to most men. The woman has taken on the man's role and is acting and thinking like a man. Men want to be men and naturally pursue. Understand, men will always remember the passiveness or aggressiveness of a woman's **pursuit**, which can lead to regret, resentment, and/or doubt regarding the relationship, especially during the challenging or hard times that are to come.

To Women...

To build a solid foundation, *ladies*, **allow** the man to pursue **without** you using **manipulation** or **seduction** (which is not always physical). The tactic of manipulation **and** seduction *can* cause a man to be drawn to a woman (*who is most likely a Want*), but it will be DUE to his experiences and issues within his soul, **NOT** the Holy Spirit. A man can initially discern these tactics and know they are not right, but he may ignore the discernment (from the Holy Spirit) due to soul issues, *sexual desires*, and impatience. "Getting a man" this way does not equate to "keeping" him or long-term happiness and respect. **In addition...**

> **"**
> ...you will not have the **God-given** grace for a man God did not ***give*** you.
> **"**

The same is true in reverse. A man will not have the *God-given* grace for a woman God did not *give* him.

Women who pursue create future trust issues with the man they are pursuing if a relationship ever evolves. They tend to wonder about *other* female Pursuers having the ability to gain his attention (such as she did herself) versus knowing he is the *type* who **must** pursue a woman he *chooses*. This concern is valid. A man who can begin a relationship after being pursued by a woman can repeat this process with a new woman after being pursued *again*. If the *new* woman's pursuit is strong and she fulfills his *wants* and/or *needs*, her efforts will most likely result in an emotional or physical affair or a new relationship.

For both males and females to build and receive trust, it is BEST to allow the order of God (*men pursue, women choose*) to take its course for the most solid foundation of trust.

The Types of Pursuits™

There are several different **types of pursuits** that produce various **sub-types of pursuits**. The *type* of pursuit demonstrated reflects one's **value** and **interest level** of the one they are *pursuing*.

Although this section can apply to a male or female Pursuer, it directly addresses the male as the Pursuer, emphasizing the order of God. (A woman's type of interest can be recognized by replacing the word "pursuit" with "interest." However, I urge men and women to read this section to recognize the pursuit type.)

Here are three types of pursuits:

- ⚭ **Godly Pursuit**
- ⚭ **Worldly Pursuit**
- ⚭ *Desire* **Denied Pursuit**

Godly Pursuit

A Godly Pursuit is **exclusive**, simply put. It is when a **man** pursues only one woman at a time. God will only *give* a man a *desire* for **one woman at a time.** Men can have multiple interests at a time (due to personal *wants*), but *Godly desire* is what separates them. God is **not** going to give a man (*or you*) a *desire* for multiple women (two or more). He is not interested in making men "players" or "serial daters" or causing them to be confused or double-minded. Nor is God the source that breeds ungodly character. God is purposeful, straightforward, and never wavering. He is Holy and Righteous in all His ways. The CLEAR GIVEAWAY of this type of pursuit is, if or when a man wants to be exclusive, he will let the woman know verbally.

The All-In Pursuit

The ***sub-type of pursuit*** produced by a Godly Pursuit is an ***All-In Pursuit***. This pursuit is when a man gives his all to impress a woman while displaying Godly character, respect, and integrity. Due to various financial circumstances, this type of effort is not solely displayed by expensive dinners, gifts, etc. But the man *will* make an effort on *his* level to show the woman the value she has to *him*. A woman will *not* feel her value is cheapened by a *lack* of effort on the man's current level of ability. In addition, the man will genuinely want to get to know the woman and without stipulations, such as sex, to ignite a deeper interest. He will make quality time to get to know her at her core (her values, interests, etc.) at a comfortable pace.

This type of pursuit does not waver. For example, you notice someone is *all-in* one day—and *not-so-much* the next. Instead, they are *all-in* daily.

Worldly Pursuit

A Worldly Pursuit is **non-exclusive**, simply put. This type of pursuit is when a man pursues multiple (two or more) women at the same time. Worldly Pursuit is a byproduct of a society's norms, family culture, and, in some cases, religious doctrines. This type of pursuit can be in the form of non-exclusive dating but not always. It can also be in the form of flirtatious exchanges (through eye contact, verbal communication, and texts), "mixed signals" (which means purposefully leading one to believe there is an interest *inconsistently*), any type of quality time, verbally expressed interest, and physical contact and exchanges (such as hand touches, small or noticeable body brushes, etc.), to name a few, with **multiple** women. Worldy Pursuits are commonly done in "secret."

God is not going to lead a man (*or you*) into a Worldly Pursuit. This type of pursuit is the result of *multiple voices* due to strategies of our enemy, Satan, in an effort to confuse and distract a man from the *Will of God and* emotionally hurt the female interest involved that is being pursued (distracting her as well).

Several ***sub-types of pursuits*** derive from the Worldly Pursuit: the ***Cheap Pursuit***, the ***Semi-Interested Pursuit,*** and the ***Lustful Pursuit***.

The Cheap Pursuit

The ***Cheap Pursuit*** is ***not*** based on financial means. It is when a man does the bare minimum to get to know the woman. Also, in some cases, there is no effort made to get to know the woman outside a commonly shared environment. This pursuit can look like sporadic (infrequent) calls, "backseat" car meetings, text-only relationships, late-night or daytime "booty calls" for sexual encounters, and a lack of effort to attain *respectable* quality time. Again, this pursuit is **not** based on how much money is spent during the pursuit but more so on a *cheapened* effort. For example, going inside an inexpensive diner for one cup of coffee is *better* than a backseat car meeting with or without coffee.

This pursuit *results* from one's **low-value** and **devalued perspective** of the woman he is pursuing, for whatever reason. The lack of value can result from the woman's ***perceived*** character and behavior, false rumors regarding the woman of interest, a sexual interest only, her financial status, a stronger interest in another woman, or others' influential opinions *received* as one's *own*. He is usually pursuing more than one woman.

In long-distance "pursuits"/relationships, the man will not make an effort to see the woman/interest in person, if ever, or engage in video calls consistently (if ever) to compensate for the distance during the *Cheap Pursuit*.

In addition, the Pursuer's words will not be reflected in actions. Again, the *Cheap Pursuit* entails the Pursuer telling the woman (*or you*) one thing, doing the bare minimum (*so she keeps some form of interest in him*), and showing little to no interest in impressing her with actions, also known as "wooing" her (meaning *blowing her mind away*). Remember, *wooing* a woman doesn't have to be expensive. It is a THOUGHTFUL action that takes **special** effort. During a *Cheap Pursuit*, a woman may receive a thoughtful *call* or *text* on a special day, such as a birthday, holiday, etc. But he does not follow up with an impressive gift or date to "woo" (impress) the woman. In some cases, the Pursuer provides expensive or inexpensive gifts. However, he does not make an effort to get to know her or may require sex to become interested in her mind, life story, beliefs, etc.

Only the woman who knows her **Kingdom worth** will recognize this type of pursuit as unacceptable immediately or after a short period of observation. Material, social, sexual, or financial gain is **not** her motivation, and her interest **will** eventually diminish. She will feel and know she is *not* valued in the highest regard.

The Semi-Interested Pursuit

The ***Semi-Interested Pursuit*** results from one dating or pursuing multiple (two or more) women simultaneously. Due to multiple interests pursued simultaneously, *his* interest becomes split between several *Options*. This pursuit creates double-mindedness, which is demonstrated through unstable and inconsistent behavior and *mixed signals*—and can lead to broken hearts. This pursuit can *look like* the *Cheap Pursuit* (doing the bare minimum) **or** the *All-In Pursuit*. He can *appear all-in* (through lavish efforts) and not be, which is a form of deception. It is *also* the result of *multiple voices* that lead one to become interested in multiple women, pursue multiple women, and ultimately lose interest from time to time (*depending on which way the wind is blowing*).

The *Semi-Interested Pursuit* is *also* the result of a man showing inconsistent interest during the "Fake Break-up" breaks. They are not fully done with the person they recently *broke-up* with—but they will convince another woman that they are—*while* keeping one foot in the door of the previous relationship. As a result, they are semi-interested. *Why*? Their interest is split and non-exclusive. They will contact one only during these temporary *breaks* they will refer to as "break-ups."

Men who engage in a half-hearted *Semi-Interested Pursuit* are *more* focused on their *wants* than what God is saying and how the Holy Spirit is directing them. The Holy Spirit wants to direct you to the *God-given Desire* only. This self-centered mindset is how we know the *Semi-Interested Pursuit* is **not** a Godly Pursuit by any means. The CLEAR GIVEAWAY of this type of pursuit is the mere fact that a woman is **not** *exclusively* pursued (the ONLY woman a man is pursuing or *entertaining* or *leading on*). This behavior will directly affect one's ability to *clearly* hear from God regarding his potential mate.

The Lustful Pursuit

The **Lustful Pursuit** is driven by lust, simply put. The male's pursuit is motivated by *sexual desire* for physical intimacy, financial gain, access to certain relationships, career advancement, prestige, food, shelter, etc., from the woman being pursued. This person usually pursues more than one woman until they "achieve" all the benefits they are seeking. They also are prone to affairs. The CLEAR GIVEAWAY of this type of pursuit (or interest from a woman) is when one or more sought-out *tangible* benefits are removed (due to set boundaries until an official commitment or marriage is attained) and the person no longer pursues.

The *Desire* Denied Pursuit

The *Desire* Denied Pursuit can be **exclusive** or **non-exclusive**. This type of pursuit is when a man is in **denial** that a specific woman is a *God-given Desire* due to deception. This man *recognizes* the *Desire*, chooses to pursue her, but is **in denial** (also by *choice*) that she is a "desire" *given* by God—**for various reasons** (such as not trusting God, fear, deception, etc.). This same woman / *Desire* is pursued due to an unexplainable *knowing* that draws the man's interest, time, etc., but the male Pursuer has not *accepted* it for what *it is*. This pursuit can look *either* Worldly (*non-exclusive, Cheap, Semi-Interested*), **or** Godly (*exclusive, All-In*), **or** both (switching back and forth between types of pursuits). The pursuit most likely will not resemble the *Lustful Pursuit* due to the man's character.

Regardless of how this type of pursuit currently *looks*, it has roots in *both* a Godly Pursuit and Worldly Pursuit. Meaning, it derives from a combination of results that reflect *both* types of pursuits. This Pursuer begins his initial pursuit on the foundation of a *God-given* "desire," whether acknowledged or not. This phase is most likely when the pursuit is *exclusive*, demonstrating the Godly Pursuit. Yet, due to the *multiple voices* (people's opinions, the enemy Satan, etc.) and the *"Process of Deception," he may begin to *entertain* multiple females (by dating, flirting or showing interest in others, etc.). The woman who is a *Desire* becomes a *non-exclusive* interest. At this point, the Pursuer is reflecting the ways of the world, the Worldly Pursuit.

(*The *Deception Process* is discussed in full detail in Chapter 12, "The Reversal Effect.")

To Men and Women, Know This...

When it comes to a person who is a *Desire*, there's really no such thing as an *"unknown" Desire (just an unaccepted one)*. When **God** *gives you* a *"desire"* (according to Psalm 37:4) for someone, you **will** know, AND you will know it is (*or was*) from Him.

Doubt, a lack of clarity, or confusion are the results of other interests (by keeping your options open) and/or *other voices* that have planted seeds of doubt and confusion as it pertains to the Will of God for your life.

Another result of *other voices* is a male Pursuer or female Pursuee becoming double-minded and *"unstable in all his [or her] ways"* (James 1:8, KJV) because he or she is trying to maintain two different mindsets pertaining to each person of interest. The CLEAR GIVEAWAY of "The *Desire* Denied Pursuit" is when an *Option* (that is *not* the *Desire*) *becomes* an interest or *remains* an interest. This can result from unmerited doubt, impatience, keeping options open, and/or allowing someone's opinion to "spark" a serious *interest* in another that was or was not there prior, *although* that person has been around. This *Other Option* is known as a *Counterfeit*.

Again, the *interest* in the *other Option* is **based** on *personal wants*, impatience, or a pursuit **influenced** by outside opinions in favor of this *Option* over *the one a man is drawn to—the Desire*.

Although the *Desire* Denied Pursuit may not be ideal for the Pursuer or Pursuee (the one pursued), at least the Pursuer is moving on the right track by pursuing! This phase can be a *good thing*! It will motivate the Pursuer (or Pursuee) to become more desperate for God in pursuit of answers, clarity, purpose, His Will, and ultimately Kingdom Purpose! If you seek God for clarity with an open heart, you WILL find it (Matthew 7:7–8), and the *Counterfeit (Option)* will be exposed. As a result, this man's pursuit will shift from the *Desire* Denied Pursuit to an All-In/Godly Pursuit.

Types of Pursuits Can Change

It *is* possible for the type of pursuit to change *midstream* from one type to another.

Here are some of the possible reasons a pursuit may change:

1. One becoming enlightened to God's ways versus man's ways—or *vice versa*
2. An increased interest in someone (the one being pursued or another person)
3. A decreased interest in someone (for various reasons, preferences, discoveries, etc., including confusion caused by manipulation or deceit [which is the "Process of Deception" discussed in Chapter 12], to name a few)
4. A person's *lack of* or *increased* "expressed" interest
5. The pursued person's *lack of* or *increased* growth in character development
6. The Pursuer's *lack of* or *increased* growth in character development
7. The *acceptance* or *rejection* of the one who is a *Need* as a *God-given Desire*
8. An increase in patience or a decrease in patience (due to unfulfilled *personal desires*) during the pursuit

God can open one's eyes to **see** who someone is or close one's eyes, impacting the interest or pursuit.

Nonetheless, it is **wise** to make *choices* based on the *current type of pursuit* experienced versus the mere *hope* of a change or *preferred type of pursuit* that may or may not come—*or* come according to God's timeline.

Side note: If *you* desired a continuous pursuit (for women) or interest (for men) and it did not happen, once you begin to seek God *or* increase your seek (quality intimate prayer time, reading the Bible consistently, listening to sermons, etc.), you may be mildly hurt or disappointed. **But** you will get over it fairly quickly because of your trust in God, your faith and understanding that He is in control with your best interest at heart **always**, and "the peace of God" experienced, "which surpasses all understanding…" that will guard your heart and your mind in Christ Jesus. (Philippians 4:7 ESV)

The Unspoken Truth About Character, Core Values & Physical Attraction

Here is the reason why pursuit and interest can change or be non-existent—but is rarely acknowledged:

Character and core values usually never supersede physical attraction.

If one is aware of another's core values and understands the importance of shared values in a potential mate…if physical attraction is not there, more likely than not, another person's qualities and traits will ***not*** supersede a lack of physical attraction. Pursuit and interest may diminish or be nonexistent.

Not caring what someone looks like and *physical attraction* are different—yet the same.

"**Not caring what someone looks like**" is simply not being *stuck* on a specific type/look and capable of loving someone who looks different from one's "normal type." They are open-minded to various looks, *but* they still have to be attracted to them, to some degree, and for the attraction to grow.

Physical attraction can grow, but it must already be at a level that would make someone want to try to increase physical attraction. **If the physical attraction is 0%, the unattracted person will not attempt to pursue or maintain an interest.** A *lack* of physical attraction for someone or for *you* is not a *bad* thing. It simply means the person is not for *you* and you're not for *them*. God's *choice* for a mate **will** be physically attracted.

In the story of Jacob, Leah, and Rachel (Genesis 29–30), it appears Jacob did not like or love Leah. He may not have even been attracted to her, although she appeared to be a "good," quality woman. Jacob slept with Leah, initially through deceit (Genesis 29:25, NIV), and had children. But he loved and had a Godly *desire* to be with Rachel; he demonstrated a Godly Pursuit for Rachel, working seven years to marry her (Genesis 29:18) and, eventually, a total of fourteen years. Leah thought having children with Jacob would make him love and desire her (Genesis 30:20), a very widespread, common mistake even today. She was a "Placeholder" for Jacob...a *wife Placeholder* at that.

A ***Placeholder*** is a person who temporarily fulfills a superficial *personal* or *lustful* desire, such as companionship, sex, etc., *until* someone "better" comes along to fulfill **more** of one's *wants* and *needs*, resulting in a stronger *desire*.

In the case of Jacob and Leah, Jacob was deceived into marrying Leah while *required* to work for the one he truly *desired*, Rachel.

Placeholders can be friends, girlfriends, boyfriends, associates, etc. Even ***deeper***, a Placeholder can even be a spouse. A deceitful person can marry you with intentions to divorce once *personal desires* are met (financial gain, children, careers, gained prestige, property, etc.).

The Lustful Pursuit (from men) and interest (from women) due to someone wanting sex, money, social status, shelter, etc., may occur—but not a Godly Pursuit or genuine interest derived from a Godly *desire*.

So, to reiterate, Godly character and core values do not supersede physical attraction (unless someone is using the person they are pursuing and showing interest in and/or until they meet and develop a relationship with the person they desire—for whatever reason).

If physical attraction is not mutual, character and core values will not keep or bring two individuals together in most ethical situations.

Here are two common choices/scenarios:

- You can be with someone who has all your physical preferences and a strong physical attraction (or sexual chemistry) and allow it to take **precedence** or **supersede** the lack of *Godly character* and shared core values.

- You can be with someone due to their *Godly character* and shared core values you are **not** even a *little* physically attracted to.

Both scenarios are not ideal.

Physical attraction *and* shared core values *and* Godly character are ideal in a lifelong, healthy marriage.

In Conclusion...

By understanding the dynamics of *preparation* and *pursuit*, you are one step closer to your destined future with the mate God chose for you.

Men, allow God to "put you to sleep" to prepare you to be the BEST man/husband you can be before and after marriage.

Women, allow God to "re-form you" to be the BEST woman/wife you can be before and after marriage.

God's process cannot be rushed, manipulated, altered, contaminated, or interrupted through distractions in order to see what God is going to do. Trust God.

If you have a *desire* to be married, allow God to orchestrate His Plan from the preparation process...to meeting the *Need* He has prepared for you...to the discovery of the one who is the *God-given Desire*...to the Godly Pursuit...and ultimately...to the marriage ceremony *and* beyond. Remember, what is the goal for Kingdom marriages? DOMINION!

CHAPTER Eight

"Falling in Love" Versus "Discovery of Love"

"Falling in Love"

A general definition for "falling in love" is to apply and allow strong feelings and emotions to develop and grow for an individual regardless of the level of the relationship. This term is usually referred to during the beginning of a relationship.

Many people experience *falling in love* multiple times in their lives. It is a common experience between two people with chemistry who invest quality time in each other, driven by emotion versus purpose. Emotions are the driving force because no boundaries are in place to protect the heart. "Falling in love" is an acceptable behavior according to societal norms; therefore, it is embraced as an ideal. Due to this mindset and belief, it is experienced by *choice*.

Consequently, it is common for those who are "*Wants*" to *fall in love* with other "*Wants*" whose decisions are driven primarily by emotions and *personal wants*. However, we can't base decisions on our *wants* because our *wants* change over time. This refers to all *wants*, whether another person's or our own.

God is love. So, in essence, *falling in love* means *falling in God*, which is safe. However, because the term is commonly used to **refer** to a *person*, falling in *people* is not safe for many reasons. People change, we change, and our *wants* and *needs* change. The *Discovery of Love* is the true process to a Kingdom marriage.

"Discovery of Love"

"Discovery of Love" means *discovery of God* in a relationship for His purpose and, in this case, as partners in marriage, also known as "Kingdom Mates." The Discovery of Love is a **process** based on a series of *deliberate choices* that leads to the *growth of Godly love*, which is the ultimate result. It is a less common experience, as most societies and cultures do not promote this process. Aware or unaware, the *Discovery of Love* process *can be* experienced, but it is less likely due to social norms that do not promote God's way to discovering a *God-given* mate.

The Discovery of Love Process™ (An Overview)

- The ***discovery of a potential mate*** is the discovery of one who is a *Need*. (Phase One)

- ***Discovering love*** is discovering God in the relationship. (Phase Two)

- A *desire* to ***accept*** the *Need* as one who can become a partner. (Phase Three)

- Next, the *choice* must be made to ***choose*** the *Need* (*as a Desire*) and advance the relationship (or not) based on a *God-given* "desire." (Phase Four)

- The end result of the process is the ***growth of Godly love for spiritual fruit***. (Phase Five)

The Discovery of Love process is the essence of God's divine plans for marriage.

Phase One: The Discovery of a Potential Mate

During Phase One, the initial introductory level of getting to know someone is followed by the "discovery of a potential mate." It is the initial draw to get to know a particular *Need*. The increased interest derives from a *Godly desire* that is NOT emotionally driven but purpose-driven. Meeting someone with a complementary purpose, suitability, mature character, and the same or very similar core values while resembling Jesus, The Christ, is a rarity. The discovery of a potential mate (*Need*) is rare (due to a lack of self-preparation and *Godly* wisdom, *not* statistics and men-to-women ratios); therefore, *discovering love* is also a rare experience (which is the next phase).

Phase Two: "Discovering Love"

God is love, and love is God. As similarly mentioned, the definition of "**discovering love**" is ***discovering God*** *in a relationship for His purpose* and, in this case, as partners in marriage (also known as "Kingdom Mates"). It is the realization of a *shared agape love* that derives from quality time, the discovery of *Godly character* (*not perfection*, discussed later in Chapter 9, "No One Is Perfect"), and an *innate desire* to pursue one (for men) or embrace one (for women) driven by purpose versus emotion. It is less immediate than *falling in love* due to controlled emotions and preset physical, emotional, and practical boundaries. Sometimes, love (who *is* God) is **unintentionally** *sought* yet *found* (discovered) according to God's Timing. And sometimes, love (who *is* God) is **deliberately** *sought* and *found* (discovered), also according to God's Timing.

The presence of God will be evident during conversations, interactions, and daily affairs experienced together, creating special, memorable *moments*. It is highly possible to recognize God's anointing during these interactions, exchanges, and *moments* (for mature Believers). These moments will serve as motivation and confirmations to proceed to the next phase.

Similar to *Wants* (who attract other *Wants*), a *Need* discovers this type of "love" with *another Need*. It is **safe** to base a decision on this *desire* for one who is a *Need* because it is an acceptable *God-given desire*, resulting in a *sober* (unemotionally driven) decision.

This process is the essence of following your spirit to God's destined choices and desires, in which you must ultimately choose from free will.

Phase Three: Accepting the "Need"

By Phase Three, *purpose* and *love (God)* are discovered by **both** *"Needs."* One *Need's* discovery of *purpose* and *love* is matched by the other *Need's* discovery of *purpose* and *love*. They both meet each other's *needs* and realize they can become a *Need* for each other. During this phase, both *Needs* **accept** and acknowledge each other as *Needs*. They embrace the *Godly desire* and *discovery* of purpose and God/love *thus far—for what it is*. Denial or doubt regarding *purpose* and *love* discovered does **not** exist. This leads to lifelong marriages.

Acceptance of *what* and *who* is *needed* and the discovery of purpose are prevalent in other scenarios and healthy relationships that create benefits—such as when a city *needs* a mayor, and the mayor *needs* the city to fulfill purpose; an employee *needs* an employer, and an employer *needs* an employee to fulfill productivity, etc. The purpose is generally *fulfilled* when each person or entity involved *chooses* to partner and produce a vision in every aspect, contributing as a *two-way street*.

The same is true with all relationships (including romantic relationships). All relationships serve a purpose. This **purpose** is *discovered* either in time or from the initial introduction. However, discovering the purpose is not enough. One must **accept** the purpose that is discovered to benefit—then *chosen*.

Phase Four: Choosing the "Need"

Next is *choosing* to allow the relationship into one's life for what it is. This is the phase in which a person who is a *Need* is revealed as one who is a *Desire*. A *desire from God* has been *given* for the *Need*, and that person has to be **chosen** as an act of obedience to God based on the *Godly desire* in their heart. Once the person has been *chosen*, he or she becomes a *Needed Want / Desire*. During this phase, the relationship *should be* clearly labeled as courting, exclusively dating, engagement/fiancé, or girlfriend/boyfriend (not a personal fan of this label for couples over twenty-four years of age).

Not Choosing a "Need"

If two *Needs* meet, they can *serve* as friends to each other (because neither is in a desperate state), and the friendship can remain intact *whether or not* the "discovery" of a potential mate is revealed or accepted by one party or another (or both). If one or both people do not choose to advance the relationship to a romantic courtship by *choice*, the two *Needs* are content with remaining friends because of the high value placed on the friendship. If the mutual decision is made to remain real friends, both *Needs* are satisfied with the nature of the friendship that also serves a specific purpose (for an allotted time/*season*).

This refers to friends who *choose not* to advance the relationship to a romantic state or courtship. Some *Needs* may respectfully discontinue the friendship and go their separate ways if the "discovery" of a potential mate is not revealed or accepted by one party or another or both. If this is the case, avoid "ghosting" (disappearing without communication). Give a brief description of your decision and true intentions moving forward, respectfully. This is acceptable in the Discovery of Love process.

<u>Phase Five: The Growth of Godly Love for "Spiritual Fruit"</u>

"Godly love" deepens and increases over time. The indicator of its *growth* is the demonstration of *spiritual fruit* (also referred to as the *"fruit of the Spirit"*), which is **love, joy, peace, patience, kindness, goodness, faithfulness, gentleness, and self-control** (Galatians 5:22–23, ESV) and are ALL actions. In addition, the *"fruit"* (all the actions) will reproduce itself into practical, tangible ways to aid one's purpose, which are also actions.

Out of all the actions, **peace** is the part of the fruit that is **extremely needed** yet can easily be overlooked and underrated. It is the part of the *fruit* that results from the presence of the other parts of the *fruit*. Peace is what our spirit *needs* to truly advance Kingdom purpose. True *peace* will *only* originate from the Holy Spirit. In the simplest terms, it is the absence of unnecessary drama. It is a spiritual result derived from maturity and a person led by the Holy Spirit. Therefore, *peace* is a *very strong* indicator of spiritual growth within a relationship, not to be overlooked.

Whether through actions such as spoken words of affirmation, inspiration, motivation, or acts of service (assistance driven by physical, mental, and emotional support), **the aid to one's purpose will be evident**. Physical support is helping with tasks. Mental support is providing motivation, inspiration, and ideas for acceleration. Emotional support is providing a listening, nonjudgmental ear and encouragement and *also* includes motivation. Spiritual support is providing prayer and edification based on God's Word and being a study partner for the Bible.

The indicator of a *lack of growth* is *actions* that **hinder** you—your purpose, your training (*of any kind…in any form*), your spiritual growth, your professional growth, your mental and emotional health, your self-esteem and self-value, and your relationships with others. These actions can derive from the other person's behaviors or *your* behaviors you initiate.

The Biblical definition of *love,* which is a part of the *spiritual fruit,* provides a clear list of *actions* that indicate whether or not *Godly love* is present. It tells you what true *love* **is** and **is not**.

> **1 CORINTHIANS 13:4-7, NIV**
>
> ⁴Love is patient, love is kind. It does not envy, it does not boast, it is not proud.
>
> ⁵It does not dishonor others, it is not self-seeking, it is not easily angered, it keeps no record of wrongs.
>
> ⁶Love does not delight in evil but rejoices with the truth.
>
> ⁷It always protects, always trusts, always hopes, always perseveres.

So let's tie it all together…. With the absence of true *Godly love*, there is no spiritual growth within the relationship. The *spiritual fruit* will be lacking or even nonexistent. This phase (The Growth of Godly Love for "Spiritual Fruit" [Phase Five]) is the final and end result of the Discovery of Love process.

The purpose of all previous phases is to produce this outcome… the "growth of Godly love" that will serve as the solid foundation for possessing DOMINION (through a long-lasting, healthy marriage).

IF you believe you have experienced all of the previous phases, yet the *spiritual fruit* is not present as the end result, you have "missed the mark" (made a common mistake). A decision (or two…or more) **did not align** with God's Will.

"Missing the Mark" in the "Discovery of Love" Process: Common Mistakes

If you are not experiencing *spiritual fruit*, it can be due to one or more *common mistakes* during the five phases of the *Discovery of Love* process.

Phase One: The Discovery of a Potential Mate

Common Mistakes

The mate you believed is a *Need* is **not** a *Need*. He or she is most likely a Self-Created *Desire Counterfeit* **or** *another* type of *Counterfeit* or *Option* type (a *Want*, a *Like*, or a *Neither*). If this phase derives from **misinterpretation** (of the person's *Option* type or your *own*, or the situation in general), **manipulation** and **deception**, or **seduction**, the other phases will be affected. The relationship will not result in the *growth of Godly love*.

Phase Two: "Discovering Love"

Common Mistakes

This phase must derive from an *innate desire* to pursue (for men) or be pursued (for women) driven by purpose. Most likely, the drive to move forward to *discover love* is *driven by emotion* versus purpose (by you, the other person, or both). The common cause for a relationship to be driven by emotion is a hurting soul (*making decisions while hurting*), a *soul tie,* or the results of sexual sin through sexual physical intimacy, etc., before the appointed time. These causes can also "blind" one from *seeing* God in a relationship or friendship.

Phase Three: Accepting the "Need"

Common Mistakes

The common mistake during this phase is simple. The person who is a *Need* has yet to be fully accepted. *Doubt* is the primary reason for the lack of acceptance. Identify the **source** of the **doubt**. The origin of the source can derive from a warning from God; a seed from your enemy, Satan; a "secret" enemy; a *soul tie* to another person; a strong or slight curiosity of *other Options*; or your *own* (or the *other* person's) undealt with soulical issues.

Issues, due to the state of one's soul, are "**blinding**" and preventing you or the *other* person (or both) from (1) accepting the *Need* and (2) embracing the "Discovering Love" phase as part of the *Discovery of Love* process.

Phase Four: Choosing the "Need"

Common Mistakes

The *choice* to advance the relationship was *"out of season,"* meaning you or the other person (or both) *chose to move forward prematurely.* There is an allotted time/"season" in which it is best to move any and all relationships forward, especially a potential mate. You (or the *other*) may have waited too long to advance the relationship, and the *mutual desire* is no longer there. A lack of trusting someone with your heart or *in* the plan of God (*once revealed*) can lead to doubt in the sincerity of a person's motives and intentions of their heart. It can also leave room to consider and be distracted by a *Counterfeit*. Subsequently, the person who is a *Need* was never *chosen* and acknowledged as a *Desire* from **God**.

The Word of God reveals "intentions of the heart" (Hebrews 4:12). The Holy Scriptures can be weighed against *anyone's actions* in *comparison* to the *Biblical definition of love* (1 Corinthians 13:4–7) to determine true intentions, character, and a person's heart, which leads to the next phase....

Phase Five: The Growth of Godly Love for "Spiritual Fruit"

Common Mistakes

An **accurate definition** of *love* is the foundation for discovering AND demonstrating *spiritual fruit* (which includes *love*) derived from the growth of *Godly love*. If *spiritual fruit* is not a result of this foundation and all the other phases, your *definition of love* is most likely *not the same as the Biblical definition*. It is tainted and needs to be examined, and your mind must be renewed in this area of understanding.

First Corinthians 13:4–8 provides a CLEAR definition of TRUE LOVE.

"Wants" Fall in Love, "Needs" Discover Love

Be mindful of self-deceit. Suppose you need to be more honest with yourself in evaluating your *own* characteristics (or those of the person of interest). In that case, you can consider yourself (or the interest) a *Need* when you (or the other person) are a *Want*.

If this is the case, *discovering love* will **not** occur. The mindset and characteristics of a *Need* lead to the perspective **required** for the *Discovery of Love* process as an experience. **Remember, discovering love is discovering God.** When your thoughts, behaviors, and decisions are primarily Spirit-led (a mindset), you are simultaneously discovering the ways of God. Therefore, *Needs* are prone to discovering love.

If you think and behave as a *Want*, you will not have the ability to make Spirit-led *choices* to properly execute the phases of the *Discovery of Love* process. You will only be prone to *falling in love*, an emotionally driven process. This also applies to the person of interest if they, too, are a *Want*.

Practical Steps for "Needs" to *Avoid* the "Falling in Love" Mindset

Society and many subcultures have taught people to label **increased emotions** and **interest** in a person as *falling in love*. As a result, in the case of two people who are *Needs*, they can mistake the *discovery of love* for *falling in love* due to previous ideologies and one's *needs* being met more strongly than usual. Therefore, it is an essential **discipline** to remind yourself before and after the "discovery" of one who is a *Desire*, that you are NOT *falling in love* but enjoying *discovering love* (within the *Discovery of Love process*). Remember, this process is the discovery of God in a situation or relationship.

As discussed in the previous chapter, thoughts must be managed during this process. Thoughts will come to mind to revert your thinking. Suppose you accept the thoughts of *falling in love* (without having a verbal rebuttal) due to the increasing interest in the person or ideal relationship—paired with this thought. In that case, your emotions will enter a dangerous place, creating an emotional *soul tie*.

Emotional hurt (versus a mild disappointment) will follow if you are not *discovered* as a *Desire* and the relationship does not progress to an engagement and, ultimately, marriage.

Simply **replace** the thought, "*I'm falling in love,*" regarding a person with…

> *I am **not** falling in love. I am open-minded to the possibility of discovering love, purpose, suitability, and compatibility.*

Verbally make this statement to yourself every time the thought comes to mind.

> **2 CORINTHIANS 10:3-5, KJV**
>
> ³For though we walk in the flesh, we do not war after the flesh:
>
> ⁴(For the weapons of our warfare are not carnal, but mighty through God to the pulling down of strong holds;)
>
> ⁵Casting down imaginations, and every high thing that exalteth itself against the knowledge of God, and bringing into captivity every thought to the obedience of Christ…

*Did God say in His Word to "fall in love" with someone? Or did He give us examples of couples with **divine purpose** who demonstrated a strong, mutual love?*

Abraham and Sarah (Genesis 12–25) served a **DIVINE PURPOSE**. The *discovery of love* was *part* of the purpose and also a bonus. Mary and Joseph (Luke 1:26–56, Matthew 1:18–24), Elizabeth and Zechariah (Luke 1:5–25), Adam and Eve (Genesis 2:4–3:24), Ruth and Boaz (Ruth 2–4), to name a few, ALL served a **DIVINE PURPOSE** that was *much* bigger than themselves, their emotions, and the excitement of experiencing fuzzy "butterflies." The purpose was DOMINION. The purpose of ALL marriages is DOMINION (*rulership in the earth*), to be fruitful and multiply, and to give God glory.

To bring balance, couples *also* existed in the Bible who brought destruction due to each person marrying the wrong person for the wrong reasons or purpose. They also had Worldly characteristics. Ahab and Jezebel (in 1 Kings 16–2 Kings 9) most likely *fell in love*, married for the wrong reasons, and caused havoc in the nation of Israel. **So choose wisely.**

In Conclusion…

Falling in love is **reserved** for your relationship with **God**, who is *love*, **not people**. If the word *love* is replaced in this phrase, it is *falling in God*. Jesus is the only one to whom it is safe to *immediately* attach our emotions and let them lead us closer to Him. It is also His Will for us to allow Him to lead our lives.

Discovering love is **reserved** for your relationships with **people**. If the word *love* is replaced in this phrase, it is *discovering God*.

Discovering love is the **discovery** of **God** *in* the relationship (or people, places, careers, etc.) that is to **serve Him** through purpose…in this case, a Kingdom marriage. It is reserved for the one who is a *Need* you are *drawn* to by an unexplainable *Godly desire*…a desire **absent** of seduction, manipulation, witchcraft, and deception—at the core. **Spiritual fruit** will always be prevalent in a Godly relationship, clearly evident—and consistently increasing.

Chapter Nine

No One Is Perfect: Don't Mistake "Needs" for "The Perfect Match"

Seeking *perfection* in a person or relationship is a common mistake. This mistake derives from people looking to **find** their *wants* and *needs* in their quest for a mate (place, career, etc.). If seeking *both* attributes simultaneously, it will be harder to distinguish "*who is who*" and "*what is what.*" One focus is better than more than one focus when making a decision.

Where is this going?

Seeking both attributes (*wants* and *needs*) at the same time can cause *Option* types to be camouflaged and misread. Those who are *Wants* can be mistaken for *Needs*…and *Needs* can be mistaken for *Wants*, etc. Primarily, it can cause a *Need* to be overlooked. No person (place or opportunity) will meet every *want* and *need* perfectly.

Although a person can have a mixture of both *Want* and *Need* characteristics, one description will always outweigh the other. However, if you are not honest regarding your observation, you will *see* what you *want* to *see* and *hear* what you *want* to *hear*.

What we *want to see* and *hear* is according to factors that **create** our *wants* and *needs*. Specifically, what you ***want to see*** and ***hear*** derives from the following:

1. Your conditioned preferences
2. Your conditioned thinking
3. A descriptive list of qualities (literal and/or subconscious)
4. The ability or inability to know and understand self, *allowing* the list to change (*as you change*)
5. Your level of patience

It's human nature to *see* what we *want to see*. When there is no clear, targeted attribute (between *wants* and *needs*), it is a natural impulse not to study, in-depth, one or the other but subconsciously seek our *wants*. However, consciously focusing on identifying our *needs* will always lead to recognizing our *wants* but not necessarily the other way around. Focusing on identifying our *wants* may cause us to overlook our primary *needs*, which are most important. Again, focusing on both *wants* and *needs* is equivalent to seeking a *perfect* person.

If this is the case, no one will be *good* enough or *perfect* enough. As a result, disappointment or impatience can lead to delusion by *seeing* and *hearing* what you want to *see* and *hear* to be in a relationship. Very skilled *Counterfeits* are Master Manipulators; they are skilled at hiding flaws to *seem* like the "perfect mate."

A way to avoid seeking "perfection" is to focus on identifying *Need* **characteristics in an individual, place, opportunity, etc., or any** *option* **in general, as well as develop** *Need* **characteristics within yourself.**

A list of perfect *wants* and *needs* (literal or subconscious) provided by *one person* equals a "perfect person." This is **deception** in its purest form since there is no such thing. Every *Option* type will have pros and cons, not to be mistaken for *non-options*. When someone isn't *perfect*, we naturally compare them to someone else.

Here are two common comparisons:

1. The pros of those who are *Needs* to the cons of those who are *Wants*
2. The pros of those who are *Wants* to the cons of those who are *Needs*

Since the *option* to invest time into *Needs*, *Wants*, or both is a *choice*, it is vital to understand the **cons** of **both** *Needs* and *Wants* are **the possession of flaws.**

Before we *dive* into understanding *flaws*, it is essential to clearly understand the distinction between *personality* and *behavior*. Here is a *crash course*:

Personality Versus Behavior

The way a person thinks in conjunction with their uniqueness creates their ***personality***. It generally cannot be changed outside of trauma.

How a person was trained, directly (intentionally) and indirectly (through subliminal and subconscious teachings), influences and creates their ***behavior***. It can be changed, modeled, shaped, or eradicated. *(I've been a behaviorist for fourteen years and counting.)*

Acceptable Flaws and Frustration

"Acceptable Flaws" are defined as a *behavior* (or set of behaviors) you do not *like* but are *willing* to live with, even if it never goes away. As a Believer, these are the behaviors you are willing to tolerate while you "pray it away." (*However, this can be dangerous if applied to ongoing abuse and can breed *more* abuse.) You *choose* to tolerate these behaviors, **not** to be mistaken as tolerating one's personality. It is not wise to *choose* to invest time in a person / *Option* whose overall personality is not *liked*.

When identifying those who are *Needs*, they *will* fulfill many of your *needs*. However, they will possess "things"/imperfections such as flaws, behaviors, and ways of thinking that will **irk, annoy,** and **disappoint** you—and be considered ***frustrating*** because of *your* own preexisting and preconditioned *wants*.

When identifying those who are *Wants*, they *will* fulfill most of your *wants*. However, they will frustrate you because your unspoken *needs* are **not** naturally met, and they **lack the capability** to meet the expressed spoken *needs*. In addition, similar to *Needs*, *Wants* will also possess behaviors and ways of thinking that will **irk, annoy, disappoint,** and **frustrate** you because of *your* own preexisting and preconditioned expectations for what *you* consider *adequate* behavior.

Some of these behaviors may not change; however, some *may* change. So don't dismiss a person for having frustrating flaws you can accept as an "imperfection" and miss out on a *God-given* opportunity or mate.

"Acceptable Flaws" vs. "Deal Breakers"

Acceptable Flaws and *Deal Breakers* are **drastically** different yet commonly treated the same.

"**Acceptable Flaws,**" as previously stated, are behaviors you don't *like* but can deal with and live with *long term*, even if they never change.

"**Deal Breakers**" are behaviors you *cannot* deal with, whether *long* or *short term*. You innately know what they are based on your **original** reaction to experiencing or witnessing these behaviors or becoming aware of them through conversation. They literally *break* the *deal* of establishing a **healthy** relationship and eventually *break* the connection, trust, and relationship, causing it to end.

Many people make the **mistake** of grouping these two sets of behaviors (Acceptable Flaws and Deal Breakers) into one category: *Acceptable Flaws*. Acceptable Flaws and Deal Breakers are **NEVER** the same! Suppose you mistakingly label a Deal Breaker as an Acceptable Flaw, especially in the *beginning* of a relationship. In that case, you are headed for a breakup or divorce *if* the relationship advances to marriage. *Why?* Because Deal Breakers generally do not change. Many people make the mistake of *tolerating* them as Acceptable Flaws **until** they reach their breaking point and can no longer live with the behavior.

So, in short,

> **NEVER move forward in a relationship with a person who demonstrates Deal Breakers.**

Acceptable Flaws *can* change, **but** if they don't, you can remain happy. Deal Breakers are more complex and harder to change and may never change, especially if they were considered acceptable (for any *length of time*) at some point in the relationship. Deal Breakers will steal your joy and overall happiness. Period. They are **harmful** to your spirit and your soul and will diminish your levels of happiness.

Avoid making excuses to *accept* Deal Breakers. Remember your TRUE worth and the healthy relationship you've envisioned.

The Art of Conflict

Regarding a relationship with a *Need*, you will still have to communicate various likes and dislikes regarding behaviors, for example, "*I really don't like how you brush me off the phone in a way I feel is mean and rude.*" Clear and honest communication *may* or *may not* result in conflict.

However, when dislikes, challenges, and disagreements arise due to imperfections, perceptions, different points of view, behaviors, etc., it is a ***GREAT*** opportunity to see how conflict is handled, dealt with, and resolved. Do not "run" from and avoid conflict. Allow conflicts to naturally occur by voicing your opinions, being yourself (who you presently are), and facing the issue(s).

Temperaments are a *major* component of compatibility and suitability, and you have a *choice* whether or not you want to deal with a particular type of temper or disposition.

Conflicts present an opportune time to carefully and intentionally observe if *temperaments* (on both ends) can be handled willingly—or not.

It is also an opportune time to see if the conflict can be handled without disrespect *(or not)*. Examples of disrespect are name-calling ("dirty fighting"), yelling, insulting, belittling, emasculating, degrading, shaming, embarrassing, physical abuse, etc.

Conflicts will also reveal whether or not a person is an "extremist," judged by their reactive behaviors. Extreme overreactions lead to erratic behavior(s) and decision-making that is drastic in nature. If this is the case, consider it a "red flag" to be watched and monitored for frequency, intensity, and breaches in the relationship. However, do not "rule out" the person / *Option*. If the person has a relationship with God (and they will if they are a *Need* or *Desire*), this is a great opportunity to see if they not only *hear* from God regarding correction and instructions but also *listen* and *do* the instructions. This type of behavior adjustment takes a cultivated relationship with the Father God, humility, and true maturity.

Some people will make permanent behavior adjustments if they reverence and strive to obey God. They can also make permanent behavior adjustments if *you* stand firm and enforce your standards for respect. Allow time to reveal and validate this change of behavior by the other person.

Pride Versus Humility

Does one's *pride* supersede *humility*? If so, this will only heighten and intensify after marriage. (Besides, change, transformation, and growth are *less necessary* to most after marriage because they already have the "grand prize"...*you!*) Pride stunts growth; humility fuels it.

Pride will prevent transformation. It deceives one from renewing their mind by the Word of God and causes them to reject Godly wisdom, subsequently remaining the same. Humility will always keep a person's heart *pliable* to learn, change, and develop Godly character while working on the imperfections they acknowledge.

Suppose the person, in fact, *can* receive and implement correction (as a form of humility). In that case, I can *guarantee* you will not be the only one in the relationship who grows and apologizes, which can be *extremely* emotionally draining over time. Trust me. I know from experience.

Get Understanding

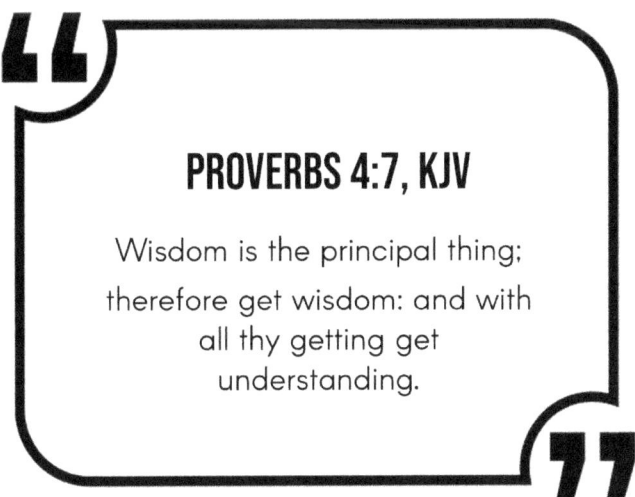

PROVERBS 4:7, KJV

Wisdom is the principal thing; therefore get wisdom: and with all thy getting get understanding.

It is wise and realistic to understand *Needs* and *Wants* both make mistakes. The difference is *Needs* handle conflict maturely (generally speaking). Their objective during a conflict is to **obtain an understanding** of a specific "train of thought," views, ideals, perspectives, etc., that **led** to a **behavior, thought process,** and **comment** by the other person. This is time well invested.

As for those who are *Wants*, they may or may not achieve the goal of reaching an understanding regarding conflicts. This is primarily due to other factors that *camouflage* relationship issues, such as sexual intimacy, a lack of communication skills, insecurities (that supersede any explanation or assurance given), or simply the *unwillingness* to achieve understanding.

Many people who are *Wants* will attempt to **avoid conflict** as if it threatens the "fantasy" relationship. When it comes to issues, they prefer to sweep them under the rug. These issues remain unresolved, and coping with unresolved issues becomes the norm. Avoidance leads to *emotional explosions* that can result in devastation (from hurtful words and/or actions) when **both** individuals do not understand the *art of conflict* and practice reaching an understanding. Conflicts will not serve their **true** purpose (*which is to obtain understanding and lead to growth*); instead, they will amount to a waste of time and energy.

Apply Patience

Mistakes and flaws are revealed over time (ideally during a courtship or while simply building a friendship). Male *Needs still* have to be chosen by the female *Needs* and vice versa. Therefore, identifying one as a *Need* does **not** create a *pass* for one not to continuously demonstrate acceptable character traits and values. With *all things being balanced*, it also does not make them exempt from mistakes. Imperfections and flaws can reveal everything one *needs* to know regarding one's *shortcomings* in a relatively short period of time, generally speaking. However, these "imperfections" should ideally be revealed over a *reasonable* length of time (3 months to 1 ½ years). This **principle of time** also applies to other areas of life requiring a major decision, such as when considering a relocation or career.

To a person who is a *Need*, the more flaws revealed, the more they develop a "take it or leave it" attitude towards the relationship. They can make a **sober** decision whether they *want* to proceed in furthering the relationship. This is *until* God reveals the person as a *Desire* (*His "stamp of approval" to move forward*) or **not** (and the person simply remains a *Need*), or the person is a *Like* (which is a crush). In either case, they can determine whether to put the interest on hold or to cease.

To a person who is a *Want*, the more flaws revealed, the more they *desire* to "help," mentor, teach, parent, coach, etc., the person of interest. These are all ***improper*** approaches to a relationship considered for marriage.

It is **vital** to determine if flaws are *acceptable* or *unacceptable*. This determination should be within the allotted time considered "reasonable" (three to nine months, generally speaking, discussed next in Chapter 10). Apply patience…but within reason.

How to Examine Flaws:

This section refers to flaws as "that thing"—as most people refer to it as. Many people will say, *"I really hate **that thing** he/she does…,"* which is generally **not** referred to as a "flaw."

The Acceptable "Thing" Versus the Unacceptable "Thing"

If the other person (or *Option*) never changed *that* one "thing" you really *don't like*, could you *really* be happy? Or are you making a decision based on a **potential** possibility of change? The reality is, *that thing* may or may never change.

If you **can** live with *that thing* **without** your overall happiness diminishing, it is an **acceptable** *thing* (also known as an Acceptable Flaw).

If you **cannot** live with *that thing* **without** feeling less than who God made you, it is an **unacceptable** *thing* (also known as a Deal Breaker).

This is the question to ask *yourself*:

"If it, 'that thing,' did not change, would 'that thing' make me constantly sad, insecure, fearful, timid, and feeling disrespected or rejected? Would it cause me to experience unhappiness frequently or even daily?"

The next "million-dollar question" to *answer* is this:

"Does 'that thing' that hurts, in some way, building you up? Or... simply tearing you down and chipping away at your self-esteem?"

If "it" (*that thing*) **is building you up**, it is "tough love" and helpful to make you a stronger Christian or person. A true friend will tell you the truth, *even* if it hurts, while loving you even more.

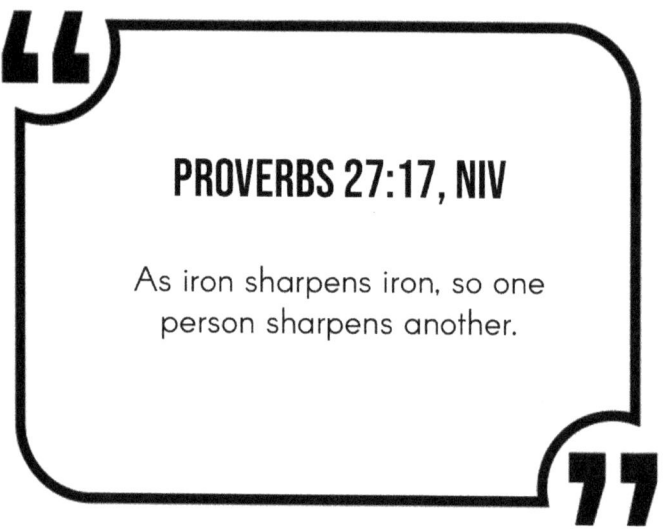

> **PROVERBS 27:17, NIV**
>
> As iron sharpens iron, so one person sharpens another.

"Iron sharpens iron..." (Proverbs 27:17, NIV) is the Word of God, so the *source* of interactions is from the **best source**—Jesus, The Christ—when a person sharpens another in righteous ways.

Truth, as painful as it may sound, yet spoken in love, will only come from Jesus, The Christ. Some areas/topics *trigger* emotional responses because they *need* to be refueled or rebuilt by Truth (known as Jesus, the Living Word of God). This spiritual and practical process will require conscious emotional control from both people in the relationship during the restoring process **and** purposeful edifying communication.

On the other hand, the enemy, Satan, will NEVER tell you Truth. He prefers for people to stay in a state of stagnation versus growing spiritually stronger, which comes from exposure and acceptance of Truth (who *is* Jesus). Jesus said, **"I Am the Truth, the Way, and the Life..." (John 14:6).**

Truth from Jesus, as the Source, will always be spoken from a place of love. However, *so-called* "truth," if not spoken in *love*—with a **pure motive**—to edify and produce life, is not Truth from God and is a deceptive lie, no matter how factual or even Biblical it may sound.

If "it" (*that thing*) is tearing you down, that person (place or thing) is *not* a viable *Option*. It may not be the time for the relationship to be explored on a courting level. Simply put, he or she is not ready. This can be due to spiritual immaturity or one (or both people) resembling *Want* / Worldy characteristics. This can also be due to a lack of sensitivity because they are still in the "sleeping" or "reforming" state (*God's process for marital preparation for development and before the wife is revealed to the husband*), such as the process of Adam and Eve in Genesis 2:21–22.

As stated in the previous chapter, "Preparation & Pursuit," while the male was *asleep* and being prepared and the female was being *reformed*, they **did not** interact (in the sense of correcting each other's flaws heavily) until God awakened them **both**.

God did not *awaken* love and romance until the appointed time. God spoke specifically to women a command through Solomon: "O daughters of Jerusalem, I adjure you: do not arouse or awaken love until the time is right" (Song of Solomon 8:4), *even* when the man expresses physical affection through touch. Song of Solomon 8:3, the verse *prior*, states, "His left hand is under my head, and his right arm embraces me." Some men will try to *only* touch, while others will try to go *further*. However, women are instructed by God not to "awaken love," which requires self-control and boundaries—if needed. The lack of this understanding of God's process and timing can cause great frustration due to **premature** intimate **interaction** (which is NOT only physical).

*__Most likely__, the person (*Option*) *tearing you down is not for you…* the *now you* or the *future you*. Remember, *that thing* may never change. It is **not wise** to move forward based on potential, especially in regard to how *you* are treated. The **source** of this behavior is **NOT**:

God…Jesus, The Christ…or the **Holy Spirit**—who are all **ONE**.

*In *extremely* rare cases, an abusive person is willing to and will change for God. Most will not. Even if they do change, it still does not mean they are the person for you. Usually they will change *after* the relationship with you or while in *another* relationship.

In Conclusion...

After identifying a person (ideally a *Need*) whom you *choose* to get to know, **do not** look for *perfection* or a flawless individual or allow the flaws to be an automatic *turnoff* (and cause you to lose interest prematurely).

Assess the flaws, and through **self-honesty**, make a decision whether *it* is something you are willing to live with *indefinitely*—or not. Keep in mind, if "it" is an Acceptable Flaw, it can possibly improve through communication and an *applied* resolution and is not a Deal Breaker. Do not make the mistake of labeling these flaws as Deal Breakers, or you can miss out on the plan of God for this potential marriage—until the opportunity comes around again with another potential mate.

Do not make a decision to tolerate a *flaw* you do not want to deal with (*and accept*) on the grounds that it *may* change because it may not. These are your Deal Breakers. Generally speaking, they are harmful to your spirit, soul, overall happiness, and health.

Every *Need* will have traits you *will* consider "*cons*." Keep this in mind as you discover these cons, and be patient for God to direct your steps.

Grant God **access** through your will and obedience, and follow His lead and directions as you **determine in your heart** to know His ways and plans. (*"Make me to know your ways, O Lord; teach me your paths."* Psalm 25:4, ESV). He will NEVER steer you wrong. *"...He leads me in the paths of righteousness for His name's sake"* (part of Psalm 23:3, ESV). **Believe Him.**

CHAPTER Ten

"Timing and Windows" & Being "Prime Enough"

This chapter specifically addresses those who are *"Needs"* and *"Desires."* Remember, to be *given* one who is a *Desire* from God, you must *first* be a person who is a *Need*. A *Need* is a person who has Godly characteristics; a *Desire* is also a person who has Godly characteristics, and God specifically *chose* them to be a mate for you.

"Timing"

It is extremely important to clearly understand "timing" according to the Word of God. This helps with *anxiousness* and irrational decision-making and aids our decision to not "settle."

God is fully in control of timing for every event in our lives that is according to His Will.

Here are a few scriptures that include the timing of God:

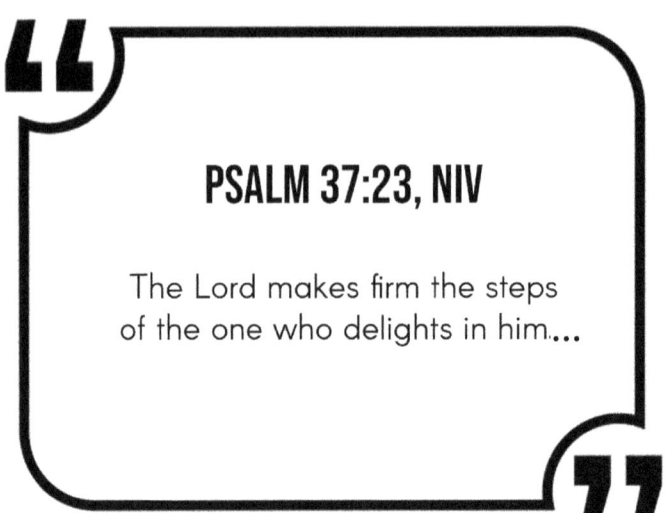

Another version states…

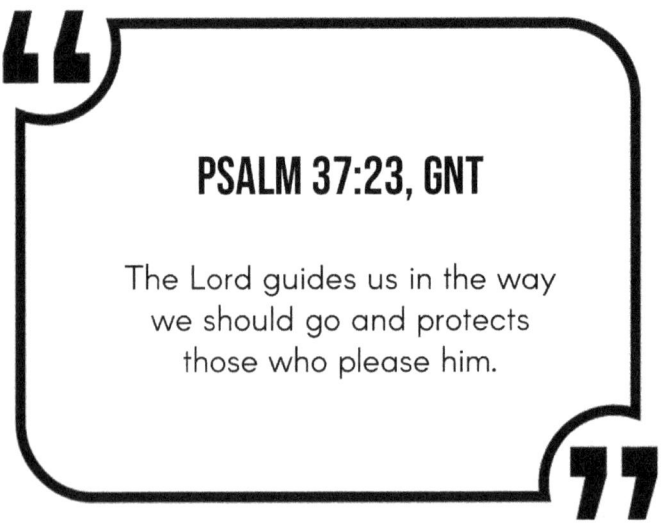

If God has already ordered ALL of our steps (Psalm 37:23) for His original plan for our lives, then He must have a **specific Will** for our lives and "the way we *should* go" (Psalm 32:8), which includes specific, strategic *timing*. Sometimes we demonstrate those steps, and sometimes we "miss the mark," altering the original plan. Because of our free will, we can *choose* to seek Him for **HIS directions** to this plan and do things His way **or** *go "our way"* on *our "own terms"* and *our "own plan"* based on *our "own timing,"* creating detours and delays. **If** we deliberately seek His Will, obey the Holy Spirit, and follow His lead, He **will** lead us to **His destined "desires,"** which **become** *our desires* (including for a potential mate) according to **His timing**. He has **already** created a specific way to allow us to experience them.

"Windows"

In the natural, a physical window can open and close. "Windows" is also a spiritual concept. They refer to opportunities available for an allotted time **only** while the *window* is open. Once the allotted time passes, the *window* closes for that particular opportunity.

There is a *window* of time to **choose** a specific person who is a *Need*. *Needs* are available during a strategically specified allotted time. They do not remain available and *optional* indefinitely. If the person (and the opportunity) is a part of God's Will, one must quickly obey the unction of the Holy Spirit to **accept** and **embrace** His Will within the *window* He *chose* to bless you with favor. This blessing includes the gift of change. Acts of obedience lead to God's blessings, a new state of being (to *be*), and a "new place." In the *new place,* another act of obedience will be required to advance to the **next** *new place* and so forth. This cycle or pattern continues throughout life. This is how we go from "faith to faith" and "glory to glory" (Romans 1:17, 2 Corinthians 3:18).

If the decision is not made to *choose* the *Need* during the open *window* of time, the *window* closes to embrace the "new" blessing. One must now wait until the next opportunity to obey the Holy Spirit (regarding a mate for marriage) presents itself again, according to God's Will and Timing.

If you miss a *window*, don't worry. The next potential mate (whether the *new* version of the same person or someone *new*) will be even *better* and more suited for the *new* you than the last person!

*God can choose *more* than one person for you!

Analyzing How Most Decide *Who* and *When* to Marry

Here's a question to think about. Generally speaking…

*Are we ultimately **basing** our decisions on the right reasons regarding **who**, **when**, and **why** to marry?*

As it pertains to marriage, the world teaches us to *choose* our mates according to the following:

- *W**ho*** and *w**hat*** will "delight" us *now*
- *W**hen*** we determine *ourselves* ready to make a lifelong decision to marry
- *H**ow*** to determine who to marry and being ready for marriage **based** on the **world's standards, our standards**, or both
- *W**hy*** to marry based on cultural norms

These layers of **deception** (to determine *who, what, when, how,* and *why* based on society's process and standards) and **erroneous teachings** (both secular and religious) *guide* **major decisions** regarding marriage… *until* the *discovery* of God's definition of "ready for marriage."

"Prime Enough": The Two Sub-Types™

There is a man-made standard and definition of being "ready" for marriage, and there is God's standard and definition of being "ready" for marriage, which I call "Prime Enough." God's "thoughts are not our thoughts," and His "ways are not our ways." His ways are higher than ours. (Isaiah 55:8–9)

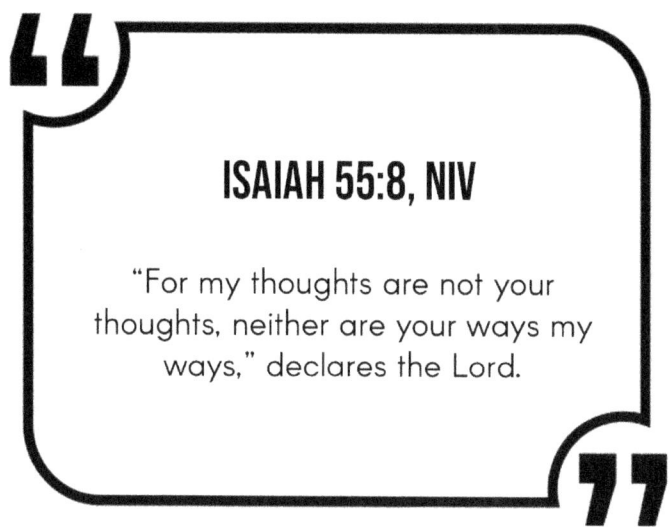

"Prime Enough" simply means God has deemed a person ready for marriage, according to His standards and timing, despite their imperfections. (They are always people who are *"Needs"* due to their maturity and character.) Being "Prime Enough" describes the blessed state of a person; for example, John Doe is "Prime Enough" and, more specifically, considered one of two sub-types.

*The two **sub-types** of Prime Enough are the "Obvious Prime Enough" and the "Not-So-Obvious Prime Enough."*

The "Obvious Prime Enough"

The characteristics of a person who is a *Need* clearly indicate being "Prime Enough" for God to advance one's life to a *desired* Kingdom marriage. *Needs*, and their *desires*, are aligned with God's Will. Therefore, *if* you are a *Need*, He can *give* you HIS specific "desire" in your heart for this area of your life, which will serve as **motivation** (*to obey, seek, commune,* and *follow Jesus, The Christ*) for the relationship.

These **noticeable** characteristics are usually due to knowledge being imparted, the manifestation of self-work, discipline, and obedience to God's Word, instructions, mentors, etc. It is a *chosen* way to conduct oneself consciously and purposefully (according to knowledge) with a deeper understanding and revelation of God's principles. This results in one being **intentionally** a Prime Enough. Their character and disposition are outwardly **obvious**; therefore, they are the "Obvious Prime Enoughs."

However, there is *another* Prime Enough that does exist. As I have examined, analyzed, and received revelational insight on other divine couples God has orchestrated for purpose, God has revealed the *other* type of *"Need"* that is ready for marriage…the *"Not-So-Obvious Prime Enough."*

The "Not-So-Obvious Prime Enough"

The Lord can consider a person Prime Enough at a *time* when he or she may not consciously be aware of their place in life (in Christ) and spiritual ranking while discovering their new self—according to purpose. God can consider one who has the **intentions** to follow and obey Him as they learn His ways, and are developing stronger, Godly characteristics (such as a *Need*) **before** they demonstrate the new attributes in their entirety. This is prior to their own knowledge and understanding of many of the Godly characteristics while learning the Word of God.

Their intentions have *yet* to be obvious outwardly. This *Need* is the "Not-So-Obvious Prime Enough." This is *when* one is operating in a dimension in which *time* has not caught up. They intend to follow God in their hearts more than they may know…but God knows.

The Word of God Will Guide Us

The following scriptures confirm God's ability to know us better than we know ourselves and what our hearts intend to do regarding adjusting our character to obey His Word.

God is the Word. The Word is a "…discerner of thoughts and intents of the heart."

> **HEBREWS 4:12, AKJV**
>
> For the word of God is quick, and powerful, and sharper than any two edged sword, piercing even to the dividing asunder of soul and spirit, and of the joints and marrow, and is a discerner of the thoughts and intents of the heart.

Before and after applying Biblical and practical knowledge to our goals, God can *read* our hearts and what we *intend* to do according to *our* plans and *knows* what we will actually *choose* to do—BEFORE the beginning of time.

> **PROVERBS 16:9, NKJV**
>
> A man's heart plans his way, But the Lord directs his steps.

He is the **Most High God** and **Almighty God** who is ALL-KNOWING.

> **1 JOHN 3:20, KJV**
>
> For if our heart condemn us, God is greater than our heart, and knoweth all things.

He knows what we *will* and *will not* do throughout time into eternity.

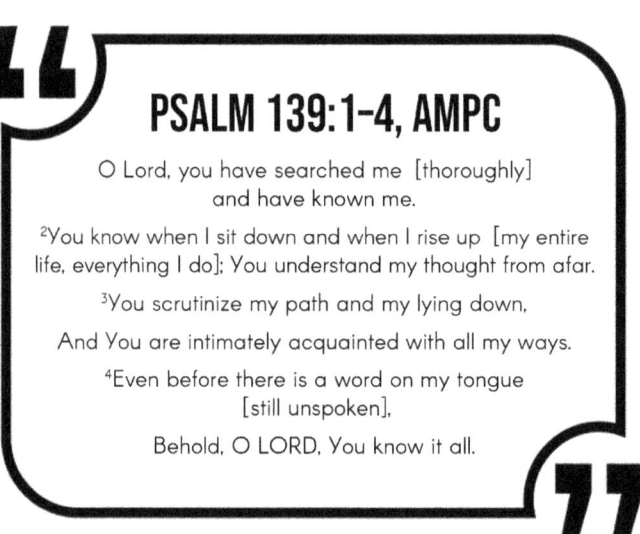

> **PSALM 139:1-4, AMPC**
>
> O Lord, you have searched me [thoroughly] and have known me.
>
> ²You know when I sit down and when I rise up [my entire life, everything I do]; You understand my thought from afar.
>
> ³You scrutinize my path and my lying down, And You are intimately acquainted with all my ways.
>
> ⁴Even before there is a word on my tongue [still unspoken],
>
> Behold, O LORD, You know it all.

When "Prime Enoughs" Collide with Time… Kingdom Couples Meet

The Lord can **consider** two of His children Prime Enough who are operating in line with His Will. When two Prime Enoughs enter into this place in life, aligned with God's Will, He will orchestrate their paths to cross and "drop" (*give*) a *desire* in each person's heart (*possibly at different times*) to PURSUE (for the *man*) and INTEREST (for the *woman*). This **encounter** is a demonstration of **God's plan**, His **timing**, and His **order**. Remember, God's plan is ALWAYS inclusive of timing and order. You **cannot** separate the three when it comes to experiencing His Will.

The Basis for Being "Prime Enough"

It is important to understand *this* section, "The Basis for Being 'Prime Enough'" **before** reading the next section, "When 'Prime Enough' *Meets* 'Prime Enough.'"

<u>Condition of the Heart</u>

Being "Prime Enough" is not based on age but on the transformation level of the heart after conversion (salvation is accepted). It also does not mean one knows all they need to know about relationships and marriage. It **means** *God has discerned the thoughts and intentions of your heart (Hebrew 4:12) and has deemed you a person who is a Need (character-wise) and a Desire for* **another** *Desire.*

Two people knowing their mate derived from God's motivation to marry each other creates a **lifelong conviction** (to **stay** married) that develops into strong endurance and aids the manifestation of purpose and DOMINION. This is God's plan for all marriages.

God is the "Ultimate Matchmaker." We simply—due to a lack of knowledge, wisdom, and revelation—go into marriages according to our ways versus His ways. Marriages built on HIS foundations and HIS ways result in lifelong marriages. Know this. Your **story** is already written. When God

orchestrated *(keyword) your marriage, He already determined the timing, discerned and approved the intentions of your heart and the other person's heart, and you're "good to go"! This is the **major** difference regarding the factors for marriage between God's way versus the world's standards. The world's standards and customs have NO way to truly discern the true motives and intentions of someone's heart and **personal desire** to marry.*

> "
> God does have a way to discern motives...and it's built systematically into His Word. Follow His Word and He will always reveal motives.
> "

*For example, if a person you are considering for marriage isn't willing to build a foundation with you without sex (as you **choose** to follow God's Word to abstain until marriage), he or she may strongly want you for sex or marry you for sex versus fulfilling God's full purpose for the marriage. This person will most likely end the relationship if this "need" isn't being fulfilled through sex because their **true** intentions weren't met, exposing their motives.*

As you start or continue to follow God's Word, for example, by abstaining from sex and waiting, the condition of one's heart and true motives will be revealed. God is a Protector.

What's most important in a marriage is both individuals living the life God ordained and giving Him glory through their testimony (that glorifies Him). This applies, ideally, before marriage and after. God must be 1st—*forever on a Throne*—to fulfill His purpose for the marriage. This requires both mates to have a heart for God.

The Holy Spirit Communicates the Same Paces

There is only one Holy Spirit. You will know if a person of interest is led by Him (the Holy Spirit) because their actions will coincide with what the Holy Spirit is telling you regarding timing. The paces will align and be the same.

*For example, (speaking to ladies only, the ones pursued) if the current month is January and the Holy Spirit has told you, "You will not be ready for a romantic relationship until November of the same year," the man who is hearing from the same Holy Spirit (regarding you and/or his own life and pace) will not pursue you until November. He may be attracted to you, drawn to you, and willing to cultivate a friendship. But he will not hear from the Holy Spirit to actively pursue (in the romantic sense) until the **appointed time** God ordained the friendship to progress to this level.*

*You will also know if a person of interest is led by the Holy Spirit because he or she will **not be in a rush to advance the relationship** when:*

1. *interest is expressed,*
2. *before or after the pursuit begins, **or***
3. *after receiving a* WORD *from God revealing a Need as a Desire from Him.*

A person (or opportunity) led by the Holy Spirit will allow the Holy Spirit to dictate the pace and lead you both. Again, the paces will align and be the same. ***There will be extreme peace and confidence along the way when the Holy Spirit begins "a thing."***

To both men and women… If you are not ready (*Prime Enough*) for marriage, the one God has for you is *also* not ready. **Stay in the process.**

> *The pace of the Holy Spirit may not always be what you **want**, but it IS what you **need**. **Desire** it.*

When "Prime Enough" *Meets* "Prime Enough"

There are three combinations, upon meeting, for *divine Kingdom couples* using the two *sub-types* of Prime Enoughs:

- 💍 "Obvious Prime Enough" *meets* "Obvious Prime Enough"
- 💍 "Not-So-Obvious Prime Enough" *meets* "Obvious Prime Enough"
- 💍 "Not-So-Obvious Prime Enough" *meets* "Not-So-Obvious Prime Enough"

"Obvious Prime Enough" *Meets* "Obvious Prime Enough"

This is the case when two people who are Prime Enoughs *meet* and **both outwardly resemble** *Need* / Godly characteristics. They are clearly *ready* for marriage, which is apparent without question. When they meet and pursue courtship, it is not "shocking."

"Not-So-Obvious Prime Enough" *Meets* "Obvious Prime Enough"

This is the case when a person becomes a *Need* fairly *quickly* according to the intentions of their heart (*which only God can read*) by doing things God's way. God then considers him or her a "Prime Enough" (a person ready for marriage), but it is *not obvious* to the average observer. This same person *becomes* a *Desire* when God *gives a Godly desire* for them—**to** an "Obvious Prime Enough's" heart. They become *Desires* to each other, following acceptance.

"Not-So-Obvious Prime Enough" *Meets* "Not-So-Obvious Prime Enough"

This is the case when *two* individuals become *Needs* rather *quickly* and discreetly. According to God's standards, they become "Prime Enough," which may *not be obvious* due to the rapid pace of transformation or because they do not *parade* their *singleness* and *devotion to God*. These two *similar Needs* meet and discover each other (as God *gives* them a *desire* for each other) and ultimately become *Desires* once the decision to receive each other is *chosen*.

In each of these cases, the divine couples are **equally yoked** *spiritually, mentally, and emotionally, whether obvious or not, according to the* **intentions of their hearts** *(not necessarily in revelation, knowledge, or healing yet). Their willingness to seek and live for God is the* **same**, *as well as most of their convictions and fundamental core values.*

In Conclusion...

The Word of God says...

> **ISAIAH 55: 8-9, NET**
>
> ⁸Indeed, my plans are not like your plans, and my deeds are not like your deeds,
>
> ⁹for just as the sky is higher than the earth, so my deeds are **superior** to your deeds and my plans **superior** to your plans.

To avoid *missing* the steps ordered by God due to your *own* plans to marry, you **must** keep an **open heart** to God's *"superior"* **plans** and "not lean to your own understanding."

Again, God is the *Ultimate Matchmaker*. **Any** combination of people **He** divinely connects is perfect because His Will is "perfect" and "acceptable" (Romans 12:2). Being *Prime Enough* is according to God, not man. Allow God to order your steps. His steps will lead you to your **divine destiny** with your *Kingdom Spouse* as one (Ephesians 5:31).

Also, remember to **trust the timing of God**. Do not try to *speed* up the timing of the process—mentally, physically, or emotionally—with the one you are led to based on emotion. Stay *purpose-driven* and *purpose-focused*. Allow the natural progression to unfold *supernaturally*. Avoid imagining the next phase of the relationship before it manifests.

On the other side of obedience is a protected heart, the perfect timing, and a Kingdom marriage to the one God *desires* for you!

CHAPTER *Eleven*

THE FIFTH AND SIXTH OPTION TYPES: "NEITHERS" & "LIKES"

So now that we have identified the *Option* types "*Wants*," "*Needs*," and "*Counterfeits*," it is **equally** as important to recognize "*Neithers*" and "*Likes*."

The "Neithers"

"*Neithers*" are simply those who are interested in *you* but you don't *want* or *need*. You don't consider them as *options* for yourself, usually through an inner witness (or "gut feeling") or preference. They also can be those who are *Wants* or *Needs* character-wise—but are not *personally desired* by you (the person *they* are interested in). The lack of *personal desire* could be due to their physical looks, personality, character, lifestyle, etc.

They will try to *appear* as those who are *Needs* because they know they're not a *Want* (in your eyes). (Remember, *Wants* are *less* mature in character but are still *wanted*.) In other words, *Neithers* will aim to appeal to your *needs* because they know they are not *wanted*. You have to be careful with *Neithers*. They try hard to spend time with you to get to know you so they can cater to your *needs* in hopes you become interested and develop a *desire* that was not originally there. They long to become (*at the least*) a *Want* but *ultimately* a *Need*—in *your* eyes. (If you *want* something long enough, you mistake it as a *need*.) In actuality, they remain a *Neither*.

Neithers also camouflage themselves as *Wants* (the type you may *personally want*), becoming the *Neither less* detected. This has a reverse effect. If a *Neither* is eventually *wanted*, they will *see* what they want to *see*—the *fantasy*—and they set *themselves* up for rejection, heartbreak, emotional hurt, and disappointment. The person who settles for a *Neither* will eventually *come to their senses*, reject the *Neither*, and always look for other *Options* (people).

Wants **strive** to become *Needs*. *Needs* **supernaturally** become *Needed Wants*. And *Needed Wants* become *Desires*. Because *Neithers* are not an *Option* for *you*, regardless of their characteristics, they simply **remain** *Neithers*.

Keep in mind, persistent *Neithers* (male or female) can become *Counterfeits* in pursuit of being with you.

Be Responsible & Accountable

It is important to recognize this *Option* for who they are and categorize them as such so he or she (or opportunity) **remains** a *Neither*.

In rare cases, the *Neither* is someone you liked or wanted (or even thought you needed) at one time, and they may have developed feelings for *you*. Don't let your feelings of not wanting to hurt the person stop you from being honest with them. The more time passes they *think* they have a *shot* at something more with you (*for whatever* they desire, good or bad), the worse the disappointment and hurt could be for them.

As you learn to recategorize *Options* (in a later chapter) and acknowledge a person as a *Neither*, it is morally ethical NOT to lead on *Neithers* because they simply are not an option for you.

What a man sows, *that* he or she will also reap.

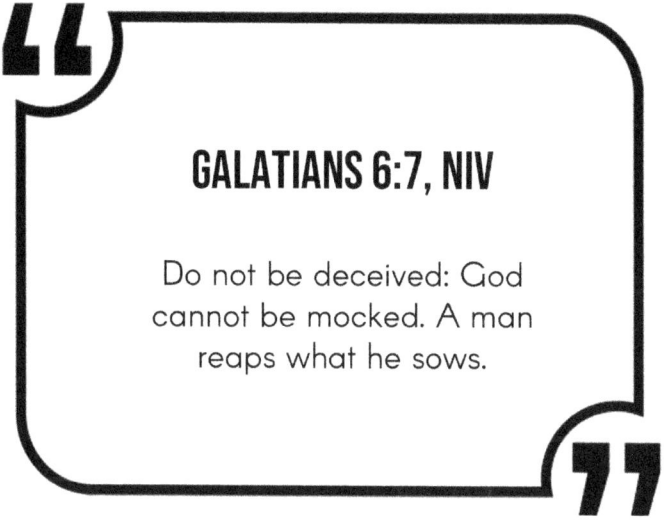

Another version of the Word of God states…

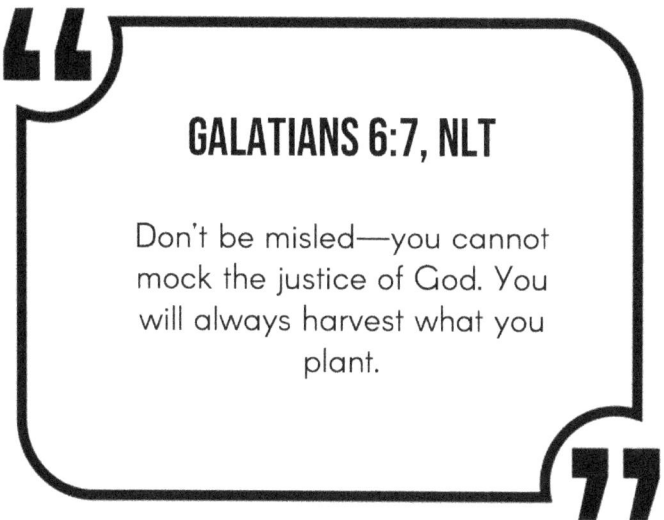

Make your disinterest clear *immediately* to uphold your integrity, spare someone's emotions, and avoid someone deceiving *you*.

The "Likes"

"*Likes*" are those you *like* (personality-wise, attracted to, etc.) and share similar interests you *like*. They may also possess similarities to what you *like* about yourself. This results in the person being *likable* according to your personal standards. You may or may not see a *next level* with them initially; however, you like them enough to, at the least, pique your interest to learn more about them beyond the surface. They are not "ruled out" from the start like *Neithers*. Instead, they are *potential* interests, also known as *Likes*. The interest in a *Like* can be slight or strong while discovering their characteristics. Think of *Likes* as "crushes."

Likes can be *Wants* or *Needs* (character-wise) or have a combination of both sets of characteristics (classifying them as *Wants*).

Needs can start out as *Likes* from the perspective "eye of the beholder" *before* discovering their characteristics categorizes them as one who is a *Need* and a *desire* is *given* for him or her by God (or not).

Likes are **not** automatically *Wants* because they may not appeal *solely* to your soulical experiences and *personal desires* or possess *Want* / Worldly characteristics. They are not automatically *Needs* because they may not *solely* appeal to your spirit and possess *Need* / Godly characteristics, per se. Yet there is *something* in particular you *like* about them. Examples of different attributes you may *like* could be one's sense of humor or charm, how they conduct business, how neat they are, one's hobbies or special interests, the conversation skills, old-fashioned chemistry and comedic rhythm shared, their physical looks, etc. Different attributes you may *like* can also be a personality trait, one (or more) of *their* interests you find yourself fascinated with, or simply a habit or discipline they possess. What you *like* has to do with the "things" you admire, appreciate, or are drawn to for pleasure and enjoyment.

Again, *Likes* can be *Wants* or *Needs*, but time spent with the person is required to know. Keep in mind *Likes* can also be *Counterfeits* if the relationship progresses (and you learn more about their character and motives).

Likes come and go. As stated, they are commonly referred to as *crushes*. Consider them for who they are—"crushes"—until more characteristics are revealed.

CHAPTER Twelve

THE REVERSAL EFFECT: WHEN "DESIRES" TURN SIMPLY INTO "WANTS" & "NEEDS"

As discussed in previous chapters, we now know that the person who is a *"Needed Want"* is the same person who is the *"Need"* God *gives* us a *heart's desire* for; the *Need* becomes a *Needed Want / Desire* once we *choose* to *accept* the *desire* from God. This person who is a *Desire* is tailored and suited for your *purpose*, *needs*, and *wants* both knowingly and unknowingly. However, suppose certain principles are **not** practiced, and boundaries are **not** established to **guard** the *Godly desire* **for** this person (who is a *Desire*) as well as the relationship. In that case, it is very common for the *Desire* to revert to one who is a *Want* or simply a *Need* in a person's mind. This can occur if thoughts (which the enemy, Satan, uses) are not strategically managed.

This chapter provides Godly wisdom and strategies to guard the plans of God from the deceptive "Reversal Effect" and willingly forfeiting God's plan for the marriage He has designed.

*Remember, the term *"Options"* refers to all *option* types/**people**:

Wants, Needs, Likes, Counterfeits, Neithers, Desires, Needed Wants / Desires.

The Process of Deception

Just because a person who is a *Need* is discovered and becomes an accepted *Desire* doesn't mean all other *Options* miraculously disappear. And these *Options*, at the least, *will* be appealing in some form. In fact, all those who are *options*, according to you, are appealing to even be *considered* an *option*. In other words, *other* appealing *Needs* and *Wants* will *still* be present, even **without** a *Godly desire* for them.

As discussed in previous chapters, the enemy, Satan, uses thoughts to derail us from the plans of God for our lives, whether a Believer (of Jesus, The Christ) or not. These thoughts pertain to "*Other Options*" that the enemy will try to make relevant and use as "Distractors."

The "Other Options"

The "*Other Option*" is **any person** (in this case, but can be a career, opportunity, relocation, etc.) who is **not** the *Desire* from God. They can be males, females, *Wants*, *Needs*, *Likes*, *Counterfeits*, or *Neithers*.

How "Other Options'" Are Used by Our Enemy AFTER the "Desire" Is Accepted

Wants are used by our enemy to be presented as suggestive, seductive *Options* to derail, delay, or cancel out purpose. They appeal primarily to our *personal wants*.

Needs can also be used by our enemy to appear and **remain** as *options* even **after** one has discovered a person who is a *Desire* from God. They can also be used to appear as an *option* even when they don't consider *themselves* an *option* for you, per se. In other words, they can *appear* as an *option* even when they're not interested in you. They appeal primarily to our *personal needs* and *purpose* (if known).

Likes (who may possess the characteristics of *Wants*, *Needs*, or both) can be used by our enemy to appeal to your ego through chemistry, fascination, admiration, and a preconceived fantasy. They appeal to *personal wants, needs,* or both on the surface.

Counterfeits (who can be *Wants* or *Needs*) are the *Other Options* who wear "masks" to get *up close and personal* and into your inner circle of influence in pursuit of a relationship with an impure motive.

Neithers can only be used to appear *as options* **if** you miscategorize them as an interest—due to a lack of self-honesty. They can be used by our enemy to waste time (entertaining a *non-option)* and cause you to plant seeds of deceit of a false interest that you will eventually reap (if not upfront and honest regarding your disinterest).

Fair Warning Regarding "Neithers"

If you are not honest regarding your disinterest and you mislead a *Neither* for self-gratification, the enemy has already begun to use you to cause a *Neither* emotional hurt and encounter a painful experience. This form of deception is an attempt to negatively shape their future perception of relationships and marriage.

*Once you have accepted the one who is your Desire, it is wise **not** to mislead **any** of these Other Options, especially Neithers. Not only will you reap what was sown—but you also can cause unnecessary emotional pain and disappointments and create experiences that can negatively impact their faith.*

One thing **all** *Other Options* have in common is…they are "**Distractors**."

Distractors

Distractors are those appealing enough to consider as a *person of interest*, even after the *Desire* is known. They are the *Other Options*.

Deception (due to *Other Options*) begins as a result of *accepting* imaginary thoughts from the enemy (about the *Other Option*[s]) that *develop* into fantasy when unchecked. Unchecked fantasy will lead to deceptive comparisons between the *Other Option* and the *Desire* you *chose* to accept from God. Once the *comparison phase* begins and completes its course, the *Other Option* will appear more appealing (Matthew 6:24) to one's *needs, wants,* and *purpose* through thoughts. *Ideal fantasizing will lead to constant comparisons that will cause the Desire / interest to* **never** *satisfy your* **expectations** *(preconceived ideals) or personal desires (wants and needs).*

Having expectations for people is never recommended.

> **Expectations are for God; 'desires' are for people.**
>
> -Dr. Matthew Stevenson, III

To bring balance, both *expectations* and *desires* for God's Will are what He requires. God's Word states, "Delight yourself in the Lord, and he will give you the **desires** of your heart" (Psalm 37:4, ESV). God's Word also states, "Therefore I say unto you, what things soever ye desire, when ye pray, **believe** that ye receive them, and ye shall have them" (Mark 11:24, KJV). These scriptures produce expectations for *Godly desires* from God, according to His Will. An example of an expectation from God (a "*Godly expectation*") is expecting a *harvest* from God due to planting/seeds sown (Genesis 8:22, NLT).

The Principle of Distractors and Idol Affection

Matthew 6:24 states, "No one can serve two masters…." "Masters" refers to anything or anyone that has our undivided attention and affection, including idols. Although the scripture refers to God and material wealth ("mammon"), the principle applies to any two opposing entities, including people.

Examples of two opposing people include a husband and a boyfriend or *side-dude*, etc. (for women), and a wife and a girlfriend, *side chick*, *side piece*, mistress, etc. (for men). They will love one and despise the other.

> **MATTHEW 6:24, AMPC**
>
> "No one can serve two masters; for either he will hate the one and love the other, or he will be devoted to the one and despise the other. You cannot serve God and mammon [money, possessions, fame, status, or whatever is valued more than the Lord]."

Once you begin to **shift attention, focus,** *and* **affection** *towards the Other Option, you will despise the one who is the Desire.*

The *Other Option* is now considered a **viable** option…*more* so than the *Desire*. This strong appeal manifests in the form of imagination and fantasy. It can derive from the fulfillment of sexual lust, false prophesies, and the opinions of trusted others (*who and what we listen to without judgment of what is being said*) through our ear gates.

Once *Other Options* are *considered* to serve the purpose of the one who is a Godly *Desire*, you will no longer view the *Desire* for who he or she is. And the *imagination* will validate *any* "red flags" and less mature or ungodly characteristics demonstrated by the *Other Options* (specifically the characteristics of *Wants*). Generally speaking, we perceive and *see* what we want to *see,* and *hear* what we want to *hear*, according to our own motives and intentions.

After marriage, this process and *train of thought* leads to divorce (legally and/or emotionally) due to emotional and physical affairs if unrecognized and unchecked according to knowledge, Godly wisdom, and the Word of God.

Distractors should *always* be placed in the No-Contact Zone (discussed in Chapter 13).

The Deception Process: How a "Desire" Digresses to a "Want" or "Need" in the Eyes of the Beholder

When you recognize and accept the one who is the *Desire* from God, the enemy, Satan, may attempt to strategically convince you they are not—through a series of thoughts—to influence your choices and derail you **away from** the perfect Will of God. This series of thoughts and actions is the Deception Process.

The Deception Process Summary

1. *Options* **remain** *options* (meaning they are still **considered** optional).
2. The enemy **uses** thoughts to cause the *Other Option(s)* to become mentally, emotionally, and physically appealing.
3. **Unchecked** imaginary **thoughts** about the *Other Option(s)* turn into (mental, emotional, and/or physical) **fantasy**.
4. The consideration of two *Options* simultaneously creates deceptive **comparisons**.
5. The enemy uses thoughts to make the *Other Option(s)* **appear** more appealing to *purpose, needs,* and *wants.*
6. The *Other Option* is **considered** to serve the purpose of the *God-given Desire.*
7. The *Godly desire* for the one who is the *Desire* becomes **questionable**.
8. The *Desire* becomes **viewed** simply as a *Need* **without** *personal desire.*
9. The *Need* **becomes** viewed as a *Want* (in the most deceptive cases).
10. The other *Option* is **pursued** (for men) or **accepted** (for women).
11. The previous *Desire* is **recategorized** as a *Need* or *Want* and placed in a Friend, Brother/Sister, Associate, Assignment, or No-Contact Zone.
12. The *Other Option* (*Need, Want,* or *Like*) **becomes** a Self-Created *Desire Counterfeit* (before *Counterfeit* traits are most likely discovered).
13. The "window" to pursue the original *Desire* **closes**.

Deception Preventative Measures

The **GREAT NEWS** is there are *preventative measures* to prevent the Deception Process from occurring and sabotaging the Will of God. Ideally, you should understand Deception Preventative Measures *before* one who is a *Desire* is revealed. If not...*well, you have this book!* Hence, part of the purpose of this book...to help you protect God's divine plans. **After** recognizing, receiving, and accepting the one who's a *Desire*, these Deception Preventive Measures should be implemented **immediately**:

- Recategorize "*Other Options*" as "Non-*Options*"
- Manage Thoughts Utilizing Scriptures
- Know Your Opponent: Common Traps Exposed

Recategorize "Other Options" as "Non-Options"

In order to prevent the Deceptive Process, you must first start by making the *choice* to view *Other Options* as non-*Options*.

Recategorize all previously considered *Options* and *new Options* (that may arise) **immediately** as non-*Options* within the appropriate Category Zone. (Use the chart in Chapter 13, "Mixed-Matched Types....") Most non-*Options* will transfer to the Associate Zone or No-Contact Zone. You should **never** place non-*Options* in the Friend Zone if they were seriously considered for marriage, you had sexual encounters with them, you shared a known strong attraction, or they were pursued (for men) at one point.

Manage Thoughts Utilizing Scriptures

Thoughts must be carefully managed to prevent comparisons between the *Desire* and *Other Options* (other *Wants*, *Needs*, and *Likes*).

The way to win and maintain control over your mind and thoughts is to MEMORIZE scriptures and use them as weapons when unethical and ungodly thoughts come to mind. When you receive thoughts to consider *Other Options* and to give them your attention, you must **immediately** quote the following scripture:

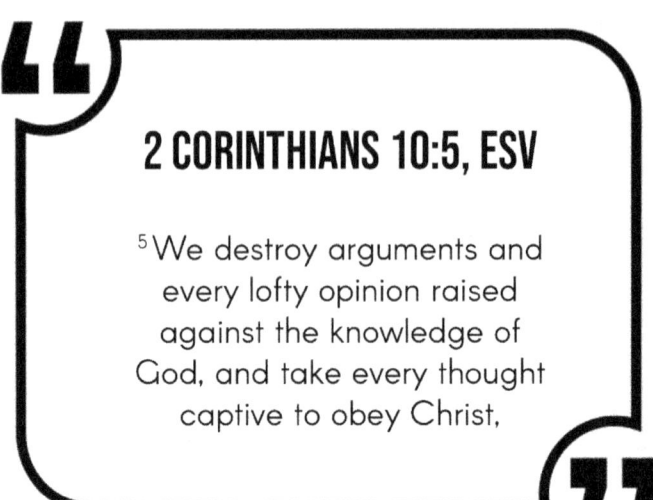

> **2 CORINTHIANS 10:5, ESV**
>
> ⁵ We destroy arguments and every lofty opinion raised against the knowledge of God, and take every thought captive to obey Christ,

Once you have memorized 2 Corinthians 10:5, continue and also memorize verses 6–7. There is no such thing as having *too many* weapons for war.

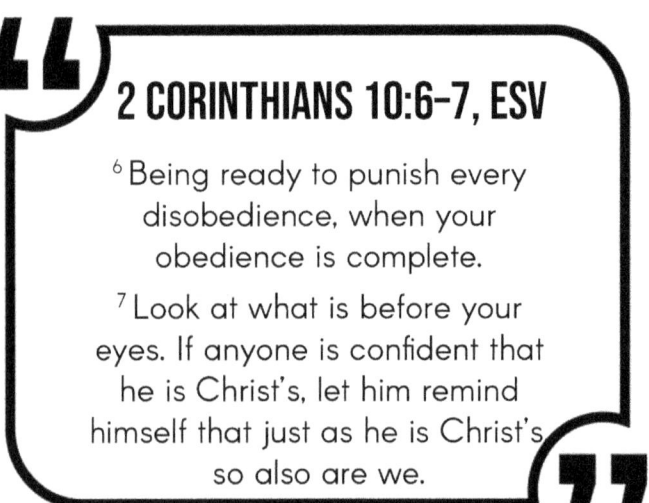

> **2 CORINTHIANS 10:6-7, ESV**
>
> ⁶ Being ready to punish every disobedience, when your obedience is complete.
>
> ⁷ Look at what is before your eyes. If anyone is confident that he is Christ's, let him remind himself that just as he is Christ's, so also are we.

The more you practice this principle of combating imaginary thoughts that are not from God with Scripture (2 Corinthians 10:5), the fewer thoughts you will receive. For short, you can also say, "I cast that down." Using the Word of God is how you avoid gaining affection for the wrong people (places or things). Practicing this principle is also how you *manage* and *control* your **mind**, **emotions**, and, ultimately, your free **will** (all part of what makes up your soul). Your **soul** must be intentionally managed.

Know Your Opponent: Common Traps Exposed

It is important to guard—I mean, TRULY guard—your eyes and ears. You cannot look at nor listen to ***anything*** that tries to replace the purpose and functions of the *Desire* or go against him or her in any form. To some, this may *seem* obvious, but the methods and strategies of the enemy, Satan, are not. Depending on one's level of spiritual maturity and understanding of Scripture, the enemy will use what *seems* like an ***Obvious Trap*** or a ***Not-So-Obvious Trap***.

"Obvious Traps" are geared towards the spiritually ***less mature*** Believer in Christ who is still learning the principles of God referring to conduct and the guidance of the Holy Spirit. A Believer is not spiritually immature because of a lack of knowledge of the Word of God in all cases. A spiritually immature Believer is one who has not fully submitted to the Lordship of Christ, meaning Christ is not the Lord of all or most decisions yet.

"Not-So-Obvious Traps" are targeted towards the spiritually ***more mature*** Believer in Christ who will not fall for (or be deceived by) the *obvious*.

Obvious Traps

Here are a *few* examples of *Obvious Traps* geared towards a spiritually ***less mature*** Believer (new to the LORDSHIP of Christ):

⚭ Through the eyes:

- Nude/partially nude pictures on social media sites
- Sex scenes in movies

💍 **Through the ears:**

- A "friend" that discusses the *Desire* in a negative light
- Degrading/ungodly music

💍 **Through the eyes and ears:**

- An *attractive* or *unattractive*, flirtatious co-worker who gains access to conduct a *personal* conversation(s)

Not-So-Obvious Traps

Here are a *few* examples of *Not-So-Obvious Traps* geared towards a spiritually **more mature** Believer:

💍 **Through the eyes:**

- A modestly dressed female Believer or gentleman Believer
- A Believer in *need* with ulterior motives

💍 **Through the ears:**

- A trusted family member who discusses the *Desire* in a negative light
- An *unattractive Counterfeit* (*Need* or *Want*) who is a Believer who gains access to conduct a *personal* conversation(s)

💍 **Through the eyes and ears:**

- An *attractive Counterfeit* (*Need* or *Want*) who is a Believer who gains access to conduct a *personal* conversation(s)

A few **scriptures** that instruct and aid our *choices* to **avoid** these *traps* that lead to derailing decisions are the following:

💍 **Proverbs 4:23** Above all else, guard your heart, for everything you do flows from it. (NIV)

- **Proverbs 4:23** Carefully guard your thoughts because they are the source of true life. (CEV)

- **Proverbs 4:24** Rid yourself of a deceitful mouth And keep devious speech far from you. (NASB)

- **1 Corinthians 15:33** Do not be misled: "Bad company corrupts good character." (NIV)

In Conclusion...

In a reverse way, deception can *creep in* to make one think if they don't receive what they *want*, they should *settle* for what they *need*. Or if they are not receiving what they *need*, they should *settle* for what they *want*.

Either way, a deceptive spirit is behind the thought, which, if acted upon, will lead to *choices* that will ultimately derail, destroy, and alter God's original plan for your life—due to a different path. These *choices*, based on deception, can lead to resentment, even if you think the *Option* (the person you settle with) is from God. If this is the case, the *Good News* is you can be restored from resentment by the Power and Anointing of God. (1Peter 5:10, Psalm 51:12, Jeremiah 30:17)

Remember, *who* and *what* God *gives* you a *desire* for will satisfy both—your Godly *wants* and *needs*. **Choosing** the one who is God's *Desire* is NEVER *settling* for second best. It is the ULTIMATE BEST and **will** propel you into destiny (the final and destined future state).

When you have arrived at this point of *choosing* God's *Desire*, that person (worthy of being *chosen*) is trustworthy for life! *Why?* Because this person is HIGHLY unlikely to be tricked or deceived out of the Will of God through others and seduction, and they have been instructed by God to be with YOU! They are tailor-made for your life journey. And guess what? They love, obey, and trust God regarding you and only need and want you! *And* God's plan for their life!

Protect this decision to *choose* the one who is God's *Desire* from all strategies of deception.

CHAPTER Thirteen

"Mixed-Matched Types": It is Very Possible

Is it possible for one person to be a "Want" and another person a "Need" in the same relationship? Absolutely! It is very possible to be "mixed-matched" in this sense. It happens all the time. *How do you know if this is the case?* The *desire* for each other will not be mutual.

The Perspective of the "Want"

The person involved in the relationship (or dating situation) who is a *Want* yet considers the other person a *Need* (as well as *themselves* in some cases) will not understand *why* the *desire* for each other is not mutual. He or she will continue to *"hold on"* until the other person *"gets it"*—referred to as the "discovery." This is the outcome of the "Planned Fantasy" syndrome (versus the God's Will/"Open Heart" mindset) referred to previously in Chapter 2, "Defining '*Wants*' and '*Needs*.'"

If the *Want* were open to God's Will and not tunnel-focused on their *planned fantasy*, they most likely would NOT be in a predicament that is *mixed-matched*. They would recognize and accept the fact that the *desire* isn't mutual. However, this capability is not a character trait of a *Want* but, in fact, a character trait of a *Need*.

The Perspective of the "Need"

Those who are *Needs* are most attracted to *Needs* due to their maturity levels. However, suppose the *Need* does not fully trust God (which requires maintenance) to supply his or her *needs* and *wants*. In that case, they will invest time into a person who is a *Want* versus remaining open-minded, patient, and in expectation for God to reveal the person who is a *Desire*. This can lead to a *mixed-matched* relationship.

The *personal desire* and interest (in the *Want*) to pursue or invest time into getting to know each other will derive from personal *wants* versus the unction (or leading) of the Holy Spirit. As a result, the *desires* from the *Need* **and** *Want*, in this *mixed-matched* case or relationship, will not *both* derive from God and, therefore, will not be mutually the same.

Only God can give the **same** *Godly desire* to two different people for each other that will be mutual. God is not cruel. He will not *give* a *desire* for a person to one **without** giving the same *desire* to the other. This *desire* does not refer to the strong "butterflies" feeling. It is not a byproduct of seduction. It is a *Godly desire* to pursue (for men), invest time (for men and women), and ultimately accept His Will by *choice*. When two types are *mixed-matched*, it is safe to say it is most likely NOT God's doing or timing nor *mutually equal desires* from HIM.

The Outcome of "Mixed-Matched Types" Exercise

Understanding this next section will provide more clarity regarding the **outcome** of a *mixed-matched Option* type. So far, we've covered how to identify *Option* types. Well…there's *another* crucial step….

After "*Option*" Types Are Identified, *Now What?*

*What do you do **next** once you've identified a person's Option type?*

Time to "Recategorize"!

Recategorizing Option types will provide the clarity you need to know "who is who" and "what is what" in your life regarding relationships.

You should know the **purpose** of every *Option* (person) and relationship. As a result, you will avoid wasted time, false hopes, and emotional setbacks. You will also know who is worth your time invested and the direction of each relationship. This exercise will assist in providing clarity for this purpose.

The Recategorizing "Options" Chart has been provided for this exercise.

The 8 Steps for Recategorizing "Options" (People)™

"Recategorizing" is simply the following:

1. **Identify** the person's *Option* **type**.
2. **Identify factors** associated with the *Option*.
3. **Place** him or her in a **category zone** (based on known facts).
4. **Implement** a **practical application(s)** to maintain the *new* approach and/or defined boundaries.
5. **Assign** a **specific allotted time** to allow the *Option* to remain in your life.
6. **Rename** the person's *Option* **type** (if applicable).
7. **Recategorize** him or her in a **NEW category zone** (if applicable) *after* the purpose is revealed in time.

Additional Step

8. **Identify** *Counterfeits* (if applicable).

Smile! There are detailed instructions for each step!

Once you have *recategorized* every *Option*, you will clearly see *who is who* and *what is what* to aid your *choices*. This is the primary objective.

Due to the vague and vast possibilities of multiple scenarios and factors that create a specific situation, there is no one "magical" or "supernatural" way to *recategorize*. The following exercise provides *mere* suggestions, generally speaking. The ULTIMATE Guider is the Holy Spirit.

Detailed Instructions: 8 Steps for the Recategorizing "Options" Chart

1. **Option Types:** Identify and write the person's *Option* type. (If unsure, review Chapters 2, 4, 6 & 11 as needed. Reread the definitions and characteristics for each type.) This is the *Option* type you *perceive* them to be, thus far, based on what you know and have observed.

   People *Option* Types™

   a. *Need* (Godly characteristics)

   b. *Want* (Worldly characteristics)

   c. *Neither* (Non-Option)

   d. *Like* (Crushes, the character is unknown)

   e. *Counterfeit* (Master Manipulator)

   f. *Desire* (God's choice)

   g. *Needed Want* (a known *Desire* not *yet* accepted)

   h. *Needed Want / Desire* (God's choice fully accepted)

   Example scenario (Step 1): You would like to be married in a year.

   (1) I met a person, and I have **identified** his/her *Option* **type** as a *Need*.

2. **Factors:** Identify factors associated with the *Option*. **These are experiences and observations and will usually "stand out"** versus *every* interaction encountered.

   Examples of Factors

   a. **Behaviors/activities** when together (examples: talk, pray, laugh, argue, sexual intimacy, dance, etc.; decreased or increased contact)

   b. **Events** experienced together (examples: dates, outings, traumatic encounters, life-changing moments, etc.)

c. **"Triggers,"** which are behaviors and words that arouse emotions (for you and the other person), such as anger, pain, sadness, joy, happiness, shame, etc.

d. **Type of quality time** (examples: communicative, sexual, flirty, ministry-based, "fellowship," businesslike, brother/sister friendly, brother/sister irritating, argumentative, combative, "easy" communication, fun, silly, youthful, etc.)

Example scenario (Steps 1–2): You would like to be married in a year.

(1) I met a person, and I have **identified** his/her *Option* **type** as a *Need*. (2) I've also identified certain **factors**....

3. **Category Zone:** Place him or her in a category zone (based on known facts).

   People Category Zones™

   a. **Friend Zone:** A person with "good" intentions towards you, not necessarily a "best friend" but can be

   b. *Neither* **Zone:** A person you realize you don't *want, need,* or *like*

   c. **Acquaintance Zone:** A person you know of but not personally; a "surface buddy"; one you may work with in some capacity

   d. **Brother/Sister Zone:** A person you are not attracted to in the romantic sense but is considered a good friend and you trust

   e. **Limited-Contact Zone:** Natural run-ins and encounters in passing (publicly only); occasional online, phone, or text contact

   f. **No-Contact Zone:** All contact is avoided; no contact or interaction; no "secret stalking" (which is following or viewing social media profiles for periodic or regular updates regarding their life or mindset)

g. **Assignment Zone:** A person who is (or possibly) in your life for a "season" (a limited time only) to help them mature and/or help you mature

⚭ *I have included **one** crucial * **warning** for the Assignment Zone at the end of this chapter.*

h. **Purpose-in-Waiting Zone:** You heard from God who your mate is but are **waiting** for him or her to (1) *receive* the same revelation or, in some cases, (2) *renounce* the revelation, or (3) *reveal* the same revelation received by telling *you*. You are waiting on one of the three **outcomes** according to God's Timing—*while* working on yourself **before** the *Godly desire* is experienced mutually (ideally), ***purpose is discovered***, and romance is kindled. The person in this zone can be a current friend, boyfriend/girlfriend, or associate. It is not contingent on the depth of the relationship. (The suggested "allotted time" to *wait* for **one** of the **three** outcomes to occur while *becoming* a BETTER you, and possibly an accepted 𝒟*esire* according to the other person, is 3–12 months.)

⚭ *I have included **five** crucial ***warnings** for the Purpose-in-Waiting Zone at the end of this chapter. These warnings (#4 and #5) are also beneficial for all courting couples/dating situations.*

i. 𝒟*esire* **Revealed Zone:** When you both have heard from God regarding being a mate to each other and are now 𝒟*esires* (to each other) by **accepting** the *"desire"* from God. During this zone, romance is kindled, and mental and emotional intimacy are explored. Yet one must wait to be married for sexual physical intimacy/sexual intercourse, ideally. During this zone, intentional pursuit with a *new* purpose (*men only*) and investing time with a *new* purpose (*men and women*) begins. The *new* purpose is to begin a Kingdom marriage. Also, during this zone, each person has *chosen* to proceed with the Discovery of Love process, discussed previously in Chapter 8.

⚭ *I have included **three** crucial ***warnings** for the 𝒟*esire* Revealed Zone at the end of this chapter. These warnings are also beneficial for all courting couples/dating situations.*

Two category zones may be possible, but select no more than two. For example, (a) Friend *Zone* and (e) Limited-Contact *Zone*.

Example scenario (Steps 1–3): You would like to be married in a year.

(1) I met a person, and I have **identified** his/her *Option* **type** as a *Need*. (2) I've also identified certain **factors** and **(3)** placed them in the Friend **Zone**.

4. **Practical Application:** Implement a practical application(s) to assist in the maintenance of the *new approach* to the relationship, the assigned category zone, and newly defined boundaries—using the *fruit of the Spirit* (which contains multiple virtues). ***Choose the part(s) of the "fruit" you must work on* and *apply*** to the situation or relationship that is lacking to achieve the *Godly* desired outcome for a healthy relationship. More than one virtue may be needed and applied. *(*Common areas that require development)* Make a note to yourself of the reason *why* you chose which *fruit(s)*.

   Fruit of the Spirit (*as individual virtues*)

   a. **Love**

   b. **Joy**

   c. ***Peace**

   d. ***Patience**

   e. ***Kindness**

   f. **Goodness**

   g. ***Faithfulness**

   h. ***Gentleness**

   i. ***Self-Control**

Example scenario (Steps 1–4): You would like to be married in a year.

(1) I met a person, and I have **identified** his/her *Option* **type** as a *Need*. (2) I've also identified certain **factors** and (3) placed them in the Friend **Zone**. (4) My **practical application**/focus is building *patience* and *self-control*.

5. **Allotted Time:** Assign a specific amount of time to an *Option* to reveal his or her purpose (or the lack thereof) in your life. This is the length of time you set to *see* if the relationship progresses to the next level towards marriage. Do not be *overly spiritual* with this step. Assign the amount of time you think is logical, according to your plans for your life. Remember, God can make ANY adjustments, shortening or extending the *allotted time* according to His plans and timing, and HE WILL (*as long as you remain open to His Will*). Start somewhere.

God may change the timing, but the *allotted time* will keep you balanced in your endeavors. It will also prevent you from putting your life on *hold* for a particular *Option* that will not (1) *change* their type **or** intentions towards you **or** (2) *choose* to obey God (*in some cases*) regarding you or in their personal life/walk with God. The allotted time will keep you from moving *too slow* or *too fast* and help you apply patience. (This step *may* **change** their purpose in your life or their *Option* type).

Allotted Time Examples

a. **4 weeks**

b. **2–4 months**

c. **3 months**

d. **6 months**

e. **1 year**

f. **NO time indefinitely** (for those who are *Neithers*, spiritual violators, abusers, etc.)

Example scenario (Steps 1–5): You would like to be married in a year.

(1) I met a person, and I have **identified** his/her *Option* **type** as a *Need*. (2) I've also identified certain **factors** and (3) placed them in the Friend **Zone**. (4) My **practical application**/focus is building *patience* and *self-control*. **(5)** I assigned the relationship an **allotted time** of 3–6 months to *discover* whether this *Option* is a *Desire* and if the relationship progresses towards courtship.

6. **Rename** *Option* **Type** (if applicable): Identify the new *Option* type and rename him or her as such. This is based on the purpose revealed after the *originally* allotted or *revised* (shortened or extended) time has passed—and/or new information learned about the person's characteristics is revealed. *This step should only be completed **after** previous chart sections.* (You will most likely have to return to this step after the assigned allotted time in the previous step.)

Renaming the *Option* may only apply to *some Options* while other *Options* remain the same type.

Renaming *Option* Type Examples

a. *Want* **to** *Need*

b. *Need* **to** *Want*

c. *Need* **to** *Need* (no change)

d. *Need* **to** *Needed Want / Desire*

e. *Need* **to** *Counterfeit*

f. *Want* **to** *Want* (no change)

g. *Like* **to** *Need*

These are only a few examples. The possible combinations for renaming *Options* are endless. The outcomes will vary. *Important point to remember: Most *Counterfeits* are *Wants* (character-wise) that first appear to be *Needs* (with the exception of the Self-Created *Desire Counterfeit* who can be a *Want* or *Need*).

(6a) If you rename the *Option* type, **notate the reason *why*.** This is very important to keep you on course, as a reminder.

*(For your own reference, go back to section #5 in the chart provided; write the **actual length of time** it took to rename or accept the Option as is.)*

Example scenario (Steps 1–6): You would like to be married in a year.

(1) I met a person, and I have **identified** his/her *Option* **type** as a *Need*. (2) I've also identified certain **factors** and (3) placed them in the Friend **Zone**. (4) My **practical application**/focus is building *patience* and *self-control*. (5) I assigned the relationship an **allotted time** of 3–6 months to *discover* whether this *Option* is a *Desire* and if the relationship progresses towards courtship.

(6) The person remains a *Need* and is not **renamed** as the attraction simmers. ***Why?***

(6a) After six months, I **realize and accept** that this person is still a *Need*, yet I have not received a *Godly desire* to invest more time (or pursue [for men only]) nor has God revealed this person as a *Desire*.

7. **Recategorize Category Zone** (if applicable): Recategorize the *Option* in a *new* category zone based on their type and all other information revealed in time.

   Recategorizing Category Zone Examples

   a. **Friend Zone** to **Assignment Zone**

   b. *Neither* **Zone** to **No-Contact Zone**

   c. **Purpose-in-Waiting Zone** to **Limited-Contact Zone**

   d. **Brother/Sister Zone** to *Desire* **Revealed Zone**

   e. **No-Contact Zone** to **Purpose-in-Waiting Zone**

*These are only a **few examples**. Similar to Step #6 (Rename Option Type), combinations for replacing Category Zones are endless. The outcomes will vary.*

Example scenario (Steps 1–7): You would like to be married in a year.

(1) I met a person, and I have **identified** his/her Option **type** as a Need. (2) I've also identified certain **factors** and (3) placed them in the Friend **Zone**. (4) My **practical application**/focus is building *patience* and *self-control*. (5) I assigned the relationship an **allotted time** of 3–6 months to *discover* whether this Option is a Desire and if the relationship progresses towards courtship.

(6) The person remains a Need and is not **renamed** as the attraction simmers. **Why?**

(6a) After six months, I **realize and accept** that this person is still a Need, yet I have not received a *Godly desire* to invest more time (or pursue [for men only]) nor has God revealed this person as a Desire.

(7) This person is **recategorized** in a ***new* category zone**, the Brother/Sister **Zone**.

Additional Step

8. **Identify** Counterfeits (if applicable): If you suspect a person of interest (Option) is a Counterfeit, write it down. One person can resemble more that one Counterfeit type.

I highly recommend trusting your "gut feeling" and staying away from this person. It will only lead to heartache, disappointment, and "wasted" time. *Although*, if you choose not to stay away, you will gain a great lesson resulting in wisdom. This step usually takes time. I don't recommend going past the allotted time unless you feel led to by the Holy Spirit.

The workbook and webcourse accompanying this book will lead you to the answers to your questions, if any.

People Counterfeit Types™

a. **The Self-Created** *Desire Counterfeit*

b. **The Hurt-Magnet** *Counterfeit*

c. **The Religious** *Counterfeit*

d. **The Business-Opportunist** *Counterfeit*

e. **The Cradle-Robber** *Counterfeit*

f. **The Narcissistic** *Counterfeit*

g. **The Refined-Thug** *Counterfeit*

h. **The Pedophile** *Counterfeit*

1.) _____ is / may be a _____

        Name   **circle one**   **Counterfeit Type**

2.) _____ is / may be a _____.

        Name   **circle one**   **Counterfeit Type**

Time to try out the Recategorize "*Options*" Chart!

BEFORE you complete the chart, **READ** the **PEOPLE CATEGORY ZONE WARNINGS** at the end of this chapter to ensure you are assessing your *Options* as correctly as possible.

The Recategorize "Options" Chart

#1 *Option* Types	#2 Factors	#3 Category Zone	#4 Practical Application (Fruit of the Spirit)	#5 Time Allotted / Actual Time	#6 Rename Option Types	#7 Replace Category Zone
Ex. *"Want"* Person A: *(NAME)*	Sexually intimate, quality time, easy and hard communication, flirty, fellowship	Limited to No Contact Zone	Self-Control	Minimum of 12 months / 10 months and 2 weeks - actual time	*Needed Want / Desire*	*Desire* Revealed Zone
Ex. *"Need"* Person B: *(NAME)*	No discovery of being a *Needed Want*, lack of personal desire for acceptance	Friend Zone	Patience	3–6 months / 6 months - actual time	*Need*	Brother / Sister Zone
Try one! ☺						
Try Two! ☺ ☺						

Once you begin filling out the chart, (1) you will receive clarity to know *who's who* and *what's what* and, (2) you will be able to identify and hold yourself accountable for resembling the "Fruit of the Spirit" that is underdeveloped and needs to be built or rebuilt.

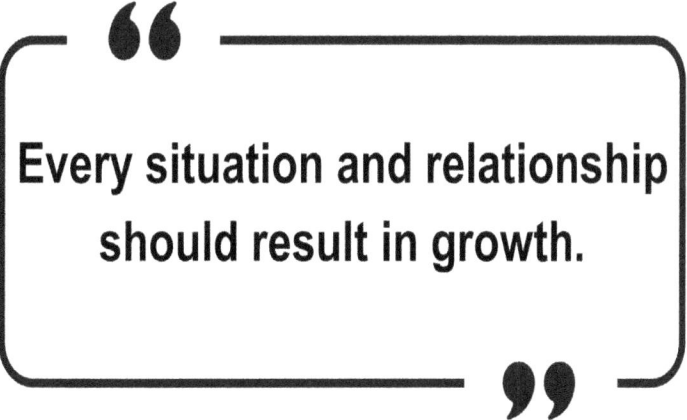

"Every situation and relationship should result in growth."

This exercise will require *extreme* honesty with self and God.

The Benefits of the Recategorizing "Options" Chart

Our *flesh* likes to rush the pace and even God's plan. Our *spirit* does not. That is why it is so important to "walk in the Spirit." *"If any man has ears to hear, let them hear"* (Mark 4:23, NKJV). Walking in the Spirit produces patience, peace, and focus, along with the other *fruit of the Spirit.*

This chart, if implemented into action, will provide solid foundations for years to come and reveal a healthy pace and perspective to apply to each situation/relationship.

In regard to marriage…. Because it is so challenging, it is very important to be REAL friends first. Friendship is the most solid foundational aspect of a lasting relationship outside of the Trinity (God, Jesus, and the Holy Spirit) as the most important.

This chart should help establish a healthy friendship either with a person who is a *Need* (until a *Godly desire* is *given* and revealed by God or *not*) OR with one who is a *Desire* while courting and "discovering love."

Identifying the people in your life or those to come will make the "process of elimination" much easier and more accurate. It will aid in the *choice-making* process to achieve your end goal: a Kingdom marriage with the right suitable mate, according to purpose, *Godly desire,* and destiny.

This chart will help you identify *who's who* and *what's what* among the *Options* (people) currently in your life OR attempting to enter your life. You should ALWAYS know the PURPOSE of EVERY individual in your life.

People Category Zone Warnings™

*Here are a few warnings regarding the **Assignment Zone**, **Purpose-in-Waiting Zone**, and **Desire Revealed Zone**.*

*Purpose-in-Waiting Zone warnings (#4 and #5) and Desire Revealed Zone warnings are useful, practical, and beneficial for all courting couples/dating situations.

*All warnings, if applied, will help you protect your peace AND the divine connection.

Assignment Zone Warning

*Warning:

Do Not Stray Away from the Purpose of the Relationship

Don't lose sight of the purpose of the Assignment Zone. If a person is in your life for a "season," let it be just that. You will know when this relationship is helping one person or the other, not naturally progressing into a romantic interest, and is most likely an "assignment" to make you better, the other person better, or both.

It is easy to allow someone in this zone to have more access than necessary or remain in your life past the appointed time. If this is done, it can tarnish the relationship, harm you (and the other person), take you off course, or become a distraction—if you stray from the purpose of the relationship. Don't make the common mistake of later placing them in the Purpose-in-Waiting Zone.

The person God has for you will not be a temporary relationship. There will not be an unction (in many cases, multiple unctions) to move on from the person who is the Desire God has for you. The time spent will not have a limit.

However, when the Assignment Zone is properly used, those in this zone will consist of temporary, time-limited relationships.

Purpose-in-Waiting Zone Warnings

*Warning #1:

Self-Honesty

*Do not see what you want to see and misuse the Purpose-in-Waiting Zone to "justify" a personal want and desire **IF** you have **not** clearly heard who your mate is from God. It will only **backfire**. The use of this zone is for those who have a relationship with Jesus, The Christ; know His voice; and* CLEARLY, *without* ANY DOUBT, *heard from the Holy Spirit regarding their potential mate. This is referred to as a "knowing." (That person is a* **potential mate** *because he or she has to choose you due to their free will.)*

*Warning #2:

A Personal "Knowing"

Your **"knowing"** CANNOT *be based on another person's "knowing," opinion, suggestion, "revelation," or prophecy. When God reveals this type of information, He will reveal it to you first* **before** *using others to confirm.*

*Warning #3 (for females only):

Be Discreet, Ladies

After using the Purpose-in-Waiting Zone, do not make suggestive hints to the male Need or inform him you heard from God regarding marriage unless unusual circumstances occur and he asks to know. However, even if he asks, only tell him IF you feel led to by the Holy Spirit. If you don't, keep it to yourself.

*Warning #4:

Stay Close to God & Wait (To Know One's Intentions)

After God tells you who your mate is, even when you notice a clear interest from that person, it is very important to remain "hidden in God" (meaning, do not respond emotionally or logically with your mouth or actions) until you know the person's true intentions. For example, conducting deep conversations about intimate personal history and family challenges, overly expressing how much you like the person, what type of sex you like, how much money you make or possess (even when asked), becoming sexually intimate, etc.

Regarding deep conversations.... Communicate a general idea of what life has taught you without the personal details. Light discussions will allow you to see (or give a general indication) if the person will potentially judge you negatively based on the deeper details of your past or embrace your history as a part of you—that contributed to your greatness and wisdom. They should embrace your life lessons and the details—at the appointed time—if they are a person who is a true *Desire*. They should have a genuine interest in learning more about you, encourage you to share, and not judge you negatively regarding the details of your story, as grimy (or not) as the details are. They should value your life story. Avoiding "deep conversations" will protect you from oversharing with a **potential mate** if you do not marry this person due to a person's free will. It will also allow time to know a person's decision whether to advance the relationship (or not) and the reason(s). You, too, may or may not choose to move forward based on what you discover. The deeper parts of your story are for your Marriage Mate.

In rare cases, such as public figures or those with publicized deep stories/testimonies, the person of interest (who is a possible *Desire*) may already know some of the intimate details of your story. Suppose the possible *Desire* proceeds with an interest (and Godly Pursuit from the man). In that case, continued interest and the positive reaction serves as a confirmation that they are tailor-made for you. He or she doesn't lose interest nor negatively judge your past. Those God called to share deep testimonies publicly will be with someone who can sincerely handle public opinion (good or bad) of their Kingdom mate/spouse. If they run or treat you less than, you've mistaken a *Counterfeit* for one who is a *Desire*; they are most likely a Self-Created *Desire Counterfeit*, at the least.

Always be mindful of your words. Your words will only dictate your actions at some point prematurely and affect emotions, good or bad. Simply acknowledge the interest and show some form of interest back—subtly, without attaching your emotions. Keep the interaction friendly and light.

The intentions of the other person (the *Needed Want*) **must be communicated** and revealed to you by him or her in a **direct manner.**

They must verbally let you know they are interested in courting or marrying you and they believe you are a Desire from God...or their husband or wife... however they choose to phrase it. This boundary will help avoid emotional letdown due to premature expectations of how you **think** *they should behave (when, where, and why) or their actual behaviors. They may demonstrate double-minded behaviors and mixed signals* **until** *either (1) obedience is fully aligned, (2) trust and faith is built to believe God's " desire" (Desire) is the BEST* **choice***, (3) purpose and revelation have been revealed, and/or (4) God's ordered steps are obeyed. (Double-mindedness derives from doubt in the wisdom from God and impatience [James 1:2–8].)*

If and when the person reveals a mutual desire and revelation from God that you are both mates, then you can safely have deeper conversations.

*Apply patience within this zone (the Purpose-in-Waiting Zone). Protect your peace and **allow God to write the unfolding story** *according to your* **choices***. The end is already completed.*

Warning #5:

Mental Self-Control

Control your imagination. Do not allow your thoughts to obsess over future goals, dreams, aspirations, and sexual intercourse with this person. It can only lead to premature behaviors, uncontrolled emotions, and heartache if the person renounces (rejects) the Will of God to be with you.

Desire Revealed Zone Warnings

Warning #1 (for couples):

Intentions & Accountability

After entering this zone (which is when both people **choose** *to proceed with the Discovery of Love process), within the first* **30** *days, it is crucial for* BOTH *parties to seek spiritual guidance (i.e., a Christ-led trustworthy pastor, etc.) for a credible witness, accountability, and wise counsel. Both individuals should be transparent, honest, and straightforward regarding their intentions and the relationship.*

Warning #2 (for couples):

Physical Touch

Within this zone, certain physical touch (kissing, holding hands, and even close hugs) is up to the conviction of the Holy Spirit. (This does not refer to sexual intercourse or intimacy, which is not an option, ideally…Biblically speaking.)

Even if only one person is convicted not to engage in certain physical touches, it is considered off limits. This is due to their season of consecration.

*A safe **boundary** for those who do not have such convictions against these acts is to restrict these physical connections to well-lit public settings only (dinner dates, social gatherings, etc.) where others are present. A clear indication that it is an act that shouldn't be experienced (even in public settings) is (1) if it tempts you to "stumble" (go further in sexual advances) or (2) you get a strong feeling of hesitation or to stop.*

*Ideally, stay away from tongue kisses regardless of the setting. The long-term **benefits** are the following:*

- *The **avoidance of temptation** of falling into sexual sin, lust, and condemnation*
- *The **protection** of the sacred relationship (between each other)*
- *The **heightened intensity** (never experienced before) of your first kiss or French kiss after marriage due to the built-up anticipation*

*The long-term benefit of these boundaries is avoiding the temptation to "plant seeds" that can sprout an unwanted harvest by straying from the Will of God that resembles holiness. **Before marriage**, trust issues, insecurities, and double-mindedness can result from premarital physical intimacy and sexual intercourse. Emotions become less controlled. In addition, trust and confidence in a person's ability to abstain from sexual desires when you are not around is unattained or affected. **After marriage**, familiarity (of lust) found within a divine and sacred connection can breed confusion and even doubt about God's revealed Will. In addition, lust, if unchecked, can lead to doubt regarding the marriage and temptation to commit adultery (physically, emotionally, or visually—such as viewing porn).*

If you do not have a conviction (an instruction from God) not to tongue kiss, avoid long kisses over five seconds to prevent going further.

Warning #3 (for couples):

The Balanced Perspective Regarding Sex Before Marriage

*This is a warning for couples **or** two individuals who believe they are Desires to each other and brought together by God, with or without a committed relationship or commitment to marry.*

When two people are committed to each other with intentions to marry, it is very common for them to feel safe enough with each other to begin sexual intimacy before the religious or civil ceremony and the possession of a marriage license. Although I highly recommend waiting until marriage, understand if you do not wait (or did not wait), it doesn't mean you cannot have a successful and blessed marriage, contrary to religious beliefs.

There are many reasons sexual intimacy can occur before a ceremony. Some people learn the order of God after sexual intercourse, after marriage, or not at all. Some people are unaware of the Biblical term "fornication" (which means any and all sexual activity outside of marriage is a sin). Some choose not to wait because of their commitment and intentions to marry. And some people want to "approve" the sexual performance before committing to a relationship or marriage. The inability to discern true motives and intentions usually leads to deception. Therefore, ***it is vitally crucial that you understand the difference between "Jumping the Gun Sex" and "Audition Sex."***

Jumping the Gun Sex™

"Jumping the Gun Sex" *occurs after a firm commitment is made between two individuals who have made a solid decision to marry based on the right reasons. They choose to have sex before marriage. However, it is still considered fornication (which is a sin) if the governing laws of the land to acknowledge a legal marriage are not yet established. (God desires us to honor the righteous laws of the land.) Yet it does not mean the union is not a divine connection. You may have just "jumped the gun" (acted prematurely).*

*I've seen plenty of married couples who were prosperous, successful, healthy, used by God, and fruitful who did not wait until marriage to have sex. The unspoken issue with this order is…**intentions are not always fulfilled and end in marriage**. Sometimes people realize the person they are engaged to (or plan to be engaged to) is not the person they will or should marry. Many key factors can be revealed to change one or both people's minds regarding marriage. However, the bond from the sexual intimacy can cause a worse pain when the engagement or relationship is severed. The safest way to know the engagement will end in marriage is to wait until the marriage is official. It is a form of major protection for your soul.*

The Biblical Understanding

The harsh reality is, tomorrow is not promised. If sexual intimacy becomes a lifestyle, you can die in sin (due to a lack of true repentance and acceptance of Jesus as Lord) before the marriage is official. Dying in sin leads to eternal damnation. This is not to scare you but to warn you…said in love (1 John 3:4, James 2:10, Jude 1:7). Revelation 21:8 says in part, regarding the "sexually immoral," their place will "be in the fiery lake of burning sulfur…." Jesus said, "My mother and my brothers are those who hear the word of God and do it" (Luke 8:21). You are not an heir of Jesus unless you hear the Word of God and actually do it.

*So let's put it all together. If you do not believe in and accept Jesus as your **Lord** and repent for your sins, you will not go where He goes…Heaven for eternity.*

*Jesus said in Matthew 7:21-23, "Not everyone who says to me, 'Lord, Lord,' will enter the kingdom of heaven, but the one who **does the will of my Father** who is in heaven." He also said, "Be doers of the word and not hearers only, deceiving yourselves" (James 1:22).*

The misconception is, if you believe in Christ, you can do what you want that pleases your soul, "repent" (for the moment) and move on…and continue the cycle. However, if you claim to believe in Christ, is He the Lord of your life? Do you allow Him to guide you…and your decisions? Many will say, "I did this…" and "I did that for you, Christ…." But did they?

Jesus said in Matthew 7:22–23, "On that day many will say to me, 'Lord, Lord, did we not prophesy in your name, and cast out demons in your name, and do many mighty works in your name?' And then will I declare to them, 'I never knew you; depart from me, you workers of lawlessness.'"

John 3:4–6 states, "Everyone who sins breaks the law; in fact, sin is lawlessness." Here is the GOOD NEWS about Jesus: "But you know that he appeared so that he might take away our sins. And in him is no sin. No one who lives in him keeps on sinning. No one who continues to sin has either seen him or known him." It takes a relationship with Jesus to hear His voice and have a heart to obey Him and do His Will; it is what He says to do that matters.

Obeying Jesus is more serious than many Believers realize and is the essence of a TRUE relationship with Him. Know Jesus by knowing His ways and allowing Him to lead you—what you do and don't do based on what HE says about it—including the area of sexual intimacy. **Truly allow Him to be your Lord.** *Experience the* **benefits***!*

Temptation is going to come…but as James 1:2–5 states, "My brethren, count it all joy when you fall into various trials, knowing that the testing of your faith produces patience. But **let patience have its perfect work, that you may be perfect and complete, lacking nothing.** *If any of you lacks wisdom, let him ask of God, who gives to all liberally and without reproach, and it will be given to him." Ask in faith, without doubting, or you'll receive nothing from the Lord, and you'll become double-minded and unstable in all your ways (James 1:6–8). We need the Lord to fight temptation.*

We all have the ability and strength to wait on sexual intimacy through the strength provided by Christ. It is simply a choice. You will "lack nothing."

Audition Sex™

*"***Audition Sex***" is when one or both individuals in a relationship (or not) have sex to impress one another or approve of the sexual performance—with or without a real established commitment. Sex becomes an unspoken "audition" before marriage or a commitment is made within one or both people's hearts to marry. (***The sexual "audition" is required to begin a committed relationship or consider marriage***.) This is the most common type of sex between unmarried people, usually referred to as "casual sex."*

For a person cunning with words and hidden motives, "Audition Sex" can be described as "Jumping the Gun Sex" to appear the same, yet it is entirely different. ("Jumping the Gun Sex" is when there is a solid commitment to marry, therefore "safe" to have sex.)

The purpose of "Audition Sex" is simply for approval. It does not lead to marriage in most cases, even if the sex is great. Why? Because no solid decision has been made to marry. Or the marriage proposal has not concluded in marriage. People change their minds for various reasons when it comes to marriage. If Audition Sex is a requirement before really getting to know each other, one or both people may realize the person is not someone they want, need, or desire to marry. This is commonly the case.

*Side note: Premarital sex can "blind" you from red flags, unsuitability, and lack of a real friendship. If you take away the sex…**what** do you both really have together…and **what** are you really dealing with? Better yet, **who** are you really dealing with?*

*Suppose one person requires Audition Sex and the other does not before marriage. The **requirement** of sex before marriage is an indication of different core values and most likely will include differences in other fundamental core values and lifestyles.*

Premarital Sex

Most people do not have the ability to discern the difference between "Jumping the Gun Sex" and "Audition Sex"; therefore, it is highly recommended to wait to have sex until the marriage is established.

Again, a great sexual relationship does not always end in marriage. But to bring balance, if there has been a serious commitment to marry and you did not wait for whatever reason, do not condemn yourselves. Do not believe the lie that you cannot move forward and be a powerful couple for God. Take steps to focus on nonsexual foundational building. These steps will not be easy, but repent before God, make a commitment to stop, set up healthy realistic boundaries to avoid temptation, purify the union, obtain a marriage license, and wait until the ceremony before continuing sexual intimacy. You will be even the more blessed for honoring God's order. You are now responsible for what you know.

My Personal Transparent Story Regarding Premarital Sex

No one is perfect, and I am no exception. After years of abstinence (not celibacy, a frequently misused word by definition), I made the mistake of trusting a man was sincere in his intentions to marry me before he truly knew me and I knew him. As a result of choosing to have premarital sex, based on serious conversations to court with the intent to marry, I ended up with a deep heartbreak without explanation. Before the heartbreak, we were still getting to know each other. Had I kept my standard, we would have learned more about each other, most likely ended the dating phase based on discoveries, and avoided the emotional pain that naturally accompanies sexual intimacy with intentions to remain together. The CLEAR GIVEAWAY this "connection" was not going to work (in hindsight) or worthy of sharing that level of intimacy was a lack of verbal expression to be in a committed relationship.

This scenario is very common. However, even when verbally agreed upon to be in an exclusive relationship, the outcome of *not* being together is highly possible as two individuals learn more about each other's flaws, character, temperaments, beliefs, core values, and personalities.

In addition, a commonly overlooked *red flag* is when another person does not accept your standards and attempts to talk you out of them. This person did just that. He did not respect my standards, beliefs, or boundaries (even though they were spiritually based) *after* attempting to justify his beliefs over mine.

Simply put, the act of disregarding a person's beliefs, standards, and values is a clear warning there are opposing fundamental values and does not equate to a foundation of respect.

At this point, I'd rather "take my chances" and wait to *sleep* with the man who is my legal husband. *Why?* Because it is NOT *taking a chance*! The lovemaking will be GREAT!

The infamous question is...

"How can one be so sure you will be sexually compatible after marriage?"

The answer is very simple. You will have a strong *knowing* the man or woman God *desires* for you is your husband or wife, the same way Eve knew who Adam was to her and Adam knew who Eve was to him. God **knows** who will satisfy you to the fullest! And that *includes* sexually! **God doesn't make mistakes!**

When two married people (including those who waited to have sex) are unfulfilled sexually, they either:

1. married the wrong person,
2. did not apply patience to get to know each other's *sexual desires*,
3. had other sexual outlets on the side (whether another sexual partner, porn, masturbation, etc.), or
4. lusted over others during the marriage, period.

Again, God doesn't make mistakes. He knows our healthy *sexual desires* and appetites. He created them and gave them to us!

> **The mate God *gives* you a *desire* for will be equally yoked sexually!**

To Men and Women…

A man or woman can say all the right things and even mean it to a certain degree. But what is equally important is their understanding of your true value and worth beyond your correctable flaws. No one wants their value trampled on or dismissed by someone who cannot see it. A man or woman who does not see your *true* value does not have what it takes to stand the test of time to love you for a lifetime.

Now, I say to you…salute the man or woman with a special thank you who made it possible for this valuable lesson to know your worth before or while reading this book full of God's Wealth and Wisdom. (I'm simply the writer; the Father God is the *true* Author.) The experience(s) may have been painful but also life-changing. In essence, he or she prepared you for your husband or wife whom you will marry after a special, beautiful, and memorable nonsexual courtship, if you so *choose*. You are far from perfect but *well* worth the wait and commitment to marriage. The only way to recognize when you are not valued is to know *your* personal value!

Know your value! Know your value! Know your value!

Now act and discern accordingly, based on *Godly wisdom*!

(If you skipped to the *Warnings section, it's time to go back to the Recategorize "Options" Chart and complete it to receive true clarity!)

Chapter Fourteen

The Power of ALL Decisions: Right, Wrong, Past, Present, and Future

Although following your spirit to destined **choices** and **desires** may be a conscious process beginning now, due to new knowledge and understanding, the story that creates your *powerful testimony* started long before you could even read this book. Therefore, ALL *choices—right, wrong, past, present, and future*—are *beneficial* AND are leading you to the new destined *choices* and "desires" God preordained for you to experience.

Along the journey, the key is to recognize the *value* in all decisions by retrieving the principles meant to be learned from the experiences and formulate wisdom to be *shared* with others. This is what makes you wise, which has no age restrictions.

Understanding the *power* of decisions will help you make *Godly solid decisions* in life and powerful *choices*, specifically regarding a potential mate; avoid paralyzing condemnation and shame; and *realize* your *God-given* power.

The Beneficial Power of ALL Decisions

The scripture that provides a clear understanding and promise that our experiences (due to *choices* or the lack thereof) will benefit us at some point in life is **Romans 8:28**.

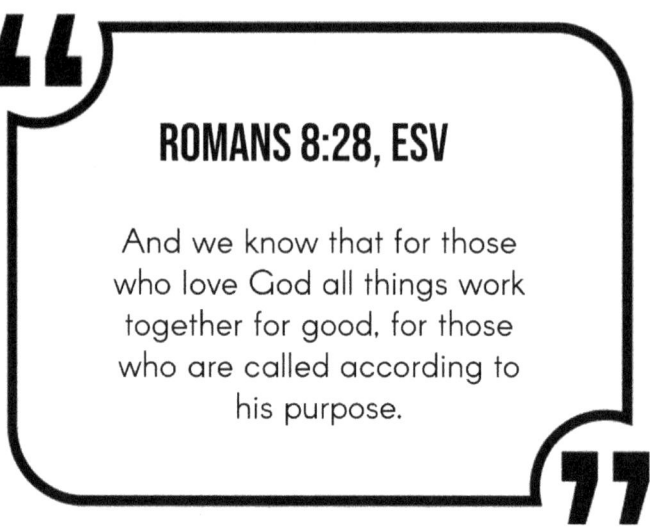

ROMANS 8:28, ESV

And we know that for those who love God all things work together for good, for those who are called according to his purpose.

This sounds great! But do not be deceived. This scripture does not apply to ALL. It clearly indicates that "all things work together for good to *THOSE* who **love** God…." This is the **1st prerequisite**.

So what does this mean?

If you don't love Christ, "all things" will NOT work together for the good. However, if you *begin* to love Christ by accepting Him (in *order* to love Him through actions of obedience), He will *supernaturally* allow your decisions—*right, wrong, past, present,* and *future*—to "work together for the ***good***." In other words, ALL decisions and experiences have the power to benefit us. This includes, but is not limited to, decisions and experiences resulting in negative (undesirable) and positive (desirable) consequences, as well as potential wisdom, providing great understanding and advancing us to a teacher, mentor, matriarch or patriarch, etc., while on Earth.

*The question to ask yourself to make life worthwhile is…

"Do you love Christ?"

The Power of Testimonies

All testimonies and life stories are FULL of mistakes. This is what makes them powerful! Transparency is the only way for others to see God in the story. The "grimier the story goes, the more of Christ the world will know"(music lyric from my song, "Greatness") *and* more of God's Glory is revealed. The lessons we learn turn our stories into powerful testimonies from mere human experiences. However,

> **...there would be no gained tailor-made lessons and wisdom if God did not allow us to make and experience the 'mistakes.'**

Protect the Testimony

Once you have a revelation (an intrusive understanding from God) regarding *how* to walk out a specific process for an allotted time, God has created and is revealing to *you* a testimony to be shared on a later date.

You MUST protect this testimony *in the making* **at ALL costs, literally**, even if it means separating from one (or many) who regularly offends (causes you to stumble) due to different lifestyles and morals. This **separation** may occur by your *choice*, theirs (for various reasons), or mere circumstances. Nevertheless, if the change protects the testimony and anointing (from offenses), it is, in fact, God! He is working *behind the scenes*. Run with it! Even if the *change* is because of manipulation by another (*regardless of their title, position, or role in* *your life*), deceit, or rejection, the overall story will become a testimony. Manipulation will never trump the Will of God. God will make **"... all things work together for good to those who love God, to those who are called according to His purpose"** (Romans 8:28). God will *use* the manipulation and/or rejection and reverse it into a form of protection for a season...*if* separation derives from it. He will reveal the source and the vessel who serves as the channel for the manipulation in time. Time never fails. I've seen truth exposed time and time again.

Protect the testimony once you have a clear understanding and instructions on *how* to walk out God's Steps. In essence, you are protecting the **POWER** it has when obedience is applied and the story is shared that will glorify God in the end.

Share! Share! Share!

As a series of *choices* formulate into a **testimony**, it is important to fulfill its **purpose**, which is to **share** it with others! With the influx of apps, social media groups, online channels, podcasts, etc., where we can share a testimony of what God did in our lives (not while it is in the making, per se), it is extremely important to share! Otherwise, only a part of its purpose has been fulfilled. This is how others are inspired by your life decisions, and principles from your story can be extracted and applied.

And let's not forget the **POWER** of sharing our stories in the form of testimonies through *old-fashioned* conversations with family members, co-workers, disciples, brothers and sisters in Christ, and selected strangers. These moments are *extremely* powerful and life-changing!

We don't share so others can duplicate our story...or even to be celebrated. We share so people can see **how** doing things "God's *way*" works! (And *not* doing things God's *way* doesn't work because it doesn't result in true joy.) We *also* share to glorify God; simultaneously, God transforms and renews the minds of others as they hear His Word in action. In the end, **God gets glorified**, simply put. God's *ways* are the principles of God that can be used interchangeably to help guide our *choices*...and, ultimately, our lives. So share, share, share!

God's Rescuing Power DENIED

Our *decisions* can lead us to various hard situations. God is capable of rescuing us out of them all—**every** situation. He *chooses* NOT to…for your growth, maturity, and purpose.

Choices have a degree of value. They are directly connected to our value system (what we perceive as valuable or invaluable). The value of each *choice* can range from a highly valuable *choice* to no value—as a *choice*. *Choices* that are considered "valuable" result in action.

> **Choices that do not have value remain *options* but do not produce action.**

*It is also a choice **not** to make a choice.*

When someone is not sure of something enough to act, they'll generally say, *"Hmmm…. That's an option…."*

What we don't *choose* to do doesn't have the amount of value it *needs* for us to act. This is because our **actions require motives**. As a behaviorist for over fifteen years, one thing I also know to be true is **every behavior/action *does* serve a function**.

A "function" is a desired outcome, motive, or end result that can lead to a lesson. The **function** could be to gain *attention, to gain *access, *self-simulation, and to *avoid or *escape. (*Reference: Applied Behavior Analysis [ABA] Functions of Behavior Concept)

I have added **additional functions**: pleasing your *flesh, soul,* and *spirit*.

The **action** we apply to produce the function is not always instinctual (*although sometimes it is*) but is learned from experiences, trial and error, or passed-on knowledge/wisdom. The "value" placed on the function, which is the desired outcome, will then motivate the *chosen* action.

Here are a few examples:

Have you ever heard someone say, "I *value* your *attention*..."? This person has placed a *high value* on the function of *****attention** and *****access** to time with that person. The *desired outcome* (which is attention and access) is the motivation to make themselves available (which is the action). Motivation is needed to take advantage of the opportunity.

Another type of example...

A person who has *chosen* to get a divorce has placed a *high value* on the function of *****escape**, which led to filing the divorce papers in court (the action). This action was motivated by a *desired outcome*: to be released from the marriage.

God gave us "free will." As discussed in previous chapters, we know we must willingly *choose* the "abundant life" and "desires" He has predestined for us to experience. However, since He cannot make us do *ANYTHING*, our actions **require** motivation.

Hard situations produce motivation and tailor our value system.

Ideally, the **lesson** God wants us to learn is (1) obtained from challenging situations, (2) motivates our *choices* towards *His Will* and *Wisdom*, and (3) shapes our behavior. For this reason, God allows us to experience the "hard" situations and does NOT rescue us (*especially when and how we think He should*). If we are "rescued," we will not learn ALL that needs to be learned for true growth.

The Missing Card Turned Life Lesson

One day, a few months after my divorce was finalized and I was rebuilding, I went to get a duplicate EBT card to replace the one I had misplaced. I parked in front of the church for a few hours after arriving early for praise dance rehearsal. I began to conduct some business over the phone, wrote the card's pin on the card sleeve, and began cleaning the car. I wanted to spend time with God in His presence, and I knew in order to hear Him clearly, I MUST clean my car. This was my personal conviction. After I cleaned, I wanted to make sure I knew where the card was before throwing anything away.

Well, I looked for the card for almost forty-five minutes to an hour and did not find it. I looked in the trunk, glove department, backpack, etc. I still could not find the card. I looked under the seats, and in the process of looking deeper for an extended length of time, I began to notice more details to clean I hadn't noticed before.

I began to find myself getting a little frustrated but *knew* this was some sort of a test or training—there was a lesson in this—simply because it really didn't *have* to be this hard (when the Holy Spirit *could* have just told me the location of the card). As I began to pick up smaller details of trash (hair, paper clips, small pieces of wrapping, etc.), I asked God, "Okay, there must be a lesson You're trying to teach me. How could it be this ***hard*** to find this card?" THEN I received the revelation! I clearly heard HIM say,

> **GOD**
>
> I allow you to go through the hard things so you can learn to clean up the small details you'd otherwise ignore.

Oh, wow! At any time, the Holy Spirit could have directed me to put the card in a specific place…or even showed me where it was right away. He didn't. BUT once I understood the lesson, He directed me *right* to the card seconds later…a hidden place under the ashtray where I would have never looked.

In other words, God allows us to stay in the hard and frustrating situations so we can learn lessons, and there are actions **we can do** while in the situation to complete a more thorough, detailed "clean up" of ourselves. The situations are there so we learn to **pay attention** to the details to fix—to make us better…and more like Him.

My car, *now more detailed than it would've been had I not had to look for the card,* is cleaner and closer to His image. My motive to clean was to hear God better, and I ended up hearing Him *so loudly*, regarding this lesson, it stopped all activity so I could acknowledge Him, His power, and His splendidness and fascinating ways! I had acknowledged in awe that He *chooses* to talk to me so clearly. This process started with me **wanting** to hear Him clearly. I *thought* I was losing time with Him by looking for the card. In actuality, I spent time *with* Him AND gained **a major experience** and **lesson** I will never forget.

"Hard situations" *reveal* **unattended details.** In other words, *hard situations* are an indication there are details God wants us to attend to.

The Child Custody "Battle"

When it comes to God's way to help us grow, all I can think of was my situation while writing a portion of this book at the beginning of the process. I was fighting a spiritual war as my children's intercessor during a painfully traumatic, hard situation. They were unlawfully taken from me through deceit to live in another state. Their residence was hidden from me for months! And I had little to no contact with them.

This extremely painful situation caused me to become a "scripture user" and "scripture memorizer" all over again. It had been years (the first few years of being *saved*, to be exact) since I had memorized the quantity of scriptures needed and used them with this high level of passion and deliberateness—as *arsenal* for something other than myself. I mean, *really* use them as arsenal! Long story short, I gained full custody, and my children were returned—with God on my side… plus the assistance of the district attorney's office and every level of law enforcement you can think of—in record time! *"Many seek the ruler's favor, But justice for man comes from the Lord" (Proverbs 29:26).*

Thank God for the "hard situations" that grew me up. This situation could've been totally avoided a million ways. But **God allowed it** so I could attend to the *details* that needed attending to—in preparation for a higher spiritual elevation and new chapter on the journey to destiny.

A few months later, I encountered *another* dramatically hard situation, and *then* I was instructed by God to start an online ministry ("TRANSPARENT 2SDAYS") in the midst of it all…. As an intercessor at *war* and a praying mother, I was well prepared and equipped to handle the hard situation God allowed while ministering to the general public. I grew leaps and bounds spiritually while obeying His Will.

God does not "rescue" us out of ALL situations so that we pay attention to details that otherwise would keep us in the same place if not corrected.

The Power of the Perceived Type of Decision

"Right" and "Wrong" Decisions

Was it wrong to not put the card away in my wallet? The answer to this question doesn't matter. Whether the answer is "yes, it *was* wrong" or "no, it *wasn't* wrong," it **led** to a *lesson*.

Your *right* **decisions** are either a result of **obedience** to God **or** based on some form of **knowledge** obtained prior. These decisions are an **intentional** act on a *choice*. Right decisions are not "guesses." A guess is just that…a guess (an *opinion* made despite uncertainty, not an action); and sometimes, a guess can influence a decision. Regardless of how you were led to a "right" decision, it is usually not confirmed as "right," so to speak, *until* after the fact…after the decision was made and acted upon.

The opposite type of decision is the same in reverse regarding "wrong" decisions. ***Wrong* decisions** are a result of **disobedience** to God **or** based on some form of **knowledge** obtained prior. (*Side note: Not all of what we know or consider "knowledge" is correct or profitable. It is simply "information" we are aware of and usually acted upon in some form.*) These decisions are also an **intentional** act on a *choice*. *Wrong* decisions are also not "guesses." Again, a guess is just that, a guess. *Wrong* decisions are based on some form of motivation and are generally not confirmed as "wrong" *until* we realize the outcome is not what we intended—*after* the decision was made and acted upon in the form of a *choice*.

We are **not** *required* to make all *right* decisions. If so, that would defeat the purpose of LIFE itself: to become dependent on Jesus and the Holy Spirit (and allow Jesus to mold and shape us to be like HIM). Instead, we are required to make *a* decision because, through movement, living, and making *choices*, we learn what we *need* to learn to **become** more like Jesus, The Christ.

Furthermore, God does not require us to make all *right choices*. God became Jesus, a man on Earth, to have a human experience *so we know* He knows what *choice-making* is like for us. Many of our *wrong choices* ultimately lead to faith in HIM, and "Faith pleases God" (Hebrews 11:6).

God is not cruel. He does not hold us "accountable" to make **certain** *choices* until we know what He wants us to know and do.

James 4:17 (NASB) states, "*So for one who knows the right thing to do and does not do it, for him it is sin.*" Jesus (through the Holy Spirit) teaches us what to do in various ways, including, but not limited to, reading the Holy Bible. He also teaches us through other people, conversations, schools, lessons, books, radio, sermons, podcasts, online videos, live videos, music, poetry…and the list goes on.

This is where the obedience factor comes in…. The only way you can consider a *choice (*or decision*) right* or *wrong* PRIOR to experiencing the outcome is to **know** what Jesus wants you to do, and you *choose* to obey or disobey. That is it. Ideally, if you don't know what the "right" thing to do is, just wait on making a *choice* until you do. If you *choose not* to wait, you will begin a detour in which you can either **learn from** or **die from** (both naturally or spiritually, indefinitely or for a *season*) to be truthful and direct.

Future Decisions

Future decisions are *choices* we made or *plan* to make but have not experienced the outcome—based on known or unknown specific details.

Known *future* decisions are the *choices* we made, in advance, before acted upon and the outcome is achieved. The choices are based on known, specific details. Common *examples* of known *future* decisions would be *New Year's resolutions*, spring goals (created before spring), quarterly goals, execution plans created in January for September goals, a planned dinner later, a marriage proposal, etc.

Here are **specific examples** of known *future* decisions:

- ⚭ You decided to marry (the decision) *Option* A, who will be the suitable mate (the choice) based on your values.

- ⚭ You decided to get a new car and you chose, specifically, car A, although you haven't purchased it yet.

Unknown *future* decisions are the *choices* we *will* make but are not considered or thought of at the present time. The details of these choices are not known nor specific. Common *examples* of unknown *future* decisions would be *chosen* mates, relocations, schools, career changes, etc. (on the larger scale), and dinner, a new car, daily schedules, outfits, etc. (on a smaller scale).

Here are **specific examples** of unknown *future* decisions:

- You decided to remarry (the decision) but you don't know who will be the suitable mate (the choice) based on your values.
- You decided to get a new car, yet you don't know which car, specifically, you will choose.

Future decisions (whether *known* or *unknown*) are byproducts of our current faith or the lack thereof. They resemble what we currently believe is possible or impossible and are highly subject to change due to unforeseen circumstances. They are, in fact, considered goals (used interchangeably) before the manifestation. They are also results of premeditations to experience a specific *desire* (from *God* or *ourselves*) or outcome through a decision. What you focus and meditate on the most will directly or indirectly shape your future decisions.

Guard Your Future Decisions

What are you meditating on?

The safest way to guard your *future* decisions is to meditate (visualize with intense thought) on the *right* things…the Word of God (what He tells us directly and through Holy Scriptures, Godly teachings, Biblical principles, assignments, prayer, etc.).

Philippians 4:8 tells us to specifically meditate on these things:

Finally, brethren, whatever things are **true**, whatever things are **noble**, whatever things are **just**, whatever things are **pure**, whatever things are **lovely**, whatever things are of **good report**, if there is any virtue and if there is anything praiseworthy—**meditate on these things.**

Future decisions become our *present* decisions once acted upon and come to fruition. The **key**, regarding *future* decisions, is **not** to decide on a *choice* until you *know* what God wants you to do.

Present Decisions

Present decisions, *to me*, are extremely fascinating to analyze out of the five types of decisions. They can derive from a *slew* of mindsets and mentalities and are directly connected to our emotions in one way or another. Yet, at the same time, we MUST make *present* decisions in order to keep living and moving—and to avoid being in *limbo* and in *discovery mode* for what type of decision (*right* or *wrong*) it will ultimately become. On the other hand, it may be best NOT to make a *present* decision if it is *unknown* what the obedient thing to do is. Remember, not making a decision is *also* a decision, and it is okay for an allotted time.

As an unemotional person in business, my *present* decisions are always based on an underlying moralistic *choice*. As a passionate person who believes in doing the *right thing* and executing ethically logical choices, the morality sought is connected to a level of emotion, although communication and execution regarding the decisions are not (and are unemotional).

Present decisions reflect our current mindset, ways of thinking, and view of life. They are byproducts of past experiences (experiential knowledge), present revelation (or the lack thereof), and intellectual knowledge, resulting in current *right* and *wrong* decisions, both knowingly and unknowingly. The *takeaway* to comprehend *present* choices is to understand this: **Present decisions produce choice behaviors that serve a specific FUNCTION, such as the following:**

- *Avoidance or escape
- *Attention
- *Self-stimulation
- **Pleasing the flesh** (*self-stimulation, physical pleasure, an act of disobedience, idol worship, etc.)

- 💍 **Pleasing the soul** (actions to feel emotionally good or bad, fantasizing, inflicting harm, helping others, mental and emotional pleasure, soul ties, an act of obedience or disobedience, idol worship, etc.)

- 💍 **Pleasing the spirit** (Godly actions to motivate self or others, an act of obedience to God, studying God's Word, worshiping Christ, etc.)

- 💍 *****Access** (*to tangibles, people, opportunities, places, God, etc.)

- 💍 *Any* combination of these listed functions

(*References: Applied Behavior Analysis [ABA] Functions of Behavior Concept by B. F. Skinner. All other concepts were originated by myself, the author of this book, through my studies and understanding of human behavior and fourteen plus years as a behavioral therapist and specialist, minister, and political scientist.)

These functions are *desired* **outcomes**…the **motivation** that drives each decision to a choice acted upon. **In short, every current/*present* decision has a motive, which is to achieve a *desired* outcome.**

The **key** to the **ideal** *present* decision-making process is *patience*. Be patient when you are unclear about what is the *right choice*. **The *right choice* will be known in *time*.**

Past Decisions

Past decisions are the *most* fascinating to me overall. *Why?* They are part of the core teachings of my ministry. There is so much undetected, uncredited VALUE in our *past* decisions that make us who we are. *Past* decisions are often a reference point for accomplishments and victories. Yet due to society's standards and culture, our past decisions are often a reference point of *shame* and *devalue*. This is a form of deception.

Past decisions are…

HIGHLY valuable and nothing to ever be ashamed of—EVER.

Simply put, *past* decisions are the MOST valuable type of decisions in our lives. They are the **core** of life's lessons that mold and shape us to become more and more like Jesus, The Christ, IF we so *choose* and *desire* to become like Him. *How is this possible? Past* decisions serve as motivation, first for change (something different…better) and ultimately transformation (permanent change). They teach us consciously and subconsciously.

Past decisions are just that…PAST decisions. They *cannot* harm you. The results can be harmful due to natural, spiritual, and legal consequences. However, the action that has already taken place is done and holds NO power *outside* of the POWER of the testimony it created. It holds no power *against* you unless you *choose* to *give* it power through the lie and deception of regret, guilt, and shame. **To be ashamed of your past is a *choice*.** Knowing the Truth (Jesus) about who you *really* are and the unimportance of others' opinions of you or your past—including *any* negative, false opinions of *yourself*—eradicates these lies and shame.

The Beauty of Mistakes

Past decisions are full of great *choices* and mistakes. Beauty comes out of them **all**…every single mistake! Whether you felt a hard or mild sting—the decision produced pain, hurt, and/or disappointment, which has the POWER to prevent you from making the same mistake again! That is a beautiful thing that is HIGHLY underrated due to the common emphasis on the actual mistake. Allow the mistake to make you better, simply put. Learn the lesson taught, and grow in maturity! Every mistake has the power to mold and shape you into a better version of yourself ***but*** under one condition: you love Jesus, The Christ.

If you love Jesus, The Christ, He promises to make all things work together for your good! And it does! I'm a living witness! What's interesting about God's Word is, if you love God, you obey God. Not perfectly—but that is your *desire* and goal. It is a *desire* that comes from Him. He is literally your Lord, meaning He directs your path and orders your steps. You must allow Him to guide you through *your* free will. Choosing to LOVE Jesus is *choosing* life more abundantly!

"Mistakes" produce seemingly "bad fruit." However, the term, *mistakes,* can also refer to what God *allows* us to do that leads to lifelong lessons despite the *bad fruit.* It will eventually benefit you and others.

You WILL see the beauty of your mistakes…sometimes immediately; sometimes it takes time. But it will happen in due season! No mistake is wasted because of the value it holds if, and only if, you *choose* to learn from it.

Personal Testimony About My Past Decisions

I slept with dozens of men in my past during my promiscuous teenage years. Society can label me as a "whore." Everyone has a backstory. What people *didn't* know is within the course of four years, one of my first "real" boyfriends passed away, and my virginity was taken by rape around the age of fourteen. Then, the first boy I *willingly* had sex with told me he was with someone else during the act when I asked, "So we're together, right?" Two male best friends I loved deeply passed away. Then, more boyfriends I loved broke my young teenage heart, appearing to use me for sex…until I gave up on having a relationship… in that order.

Sex became merely a physical act for pleasure and benefits. I began using men for what I could get…the way I felt they were using me. I didn't know Jesus personally—nor did I grow up knowing premarital sex was a sin and to abstain until marriage.

Then, around my eighteenth birthday, while pregnant, I met Jesus, and life permanently changed. I got "saved" (converted) by accepting Jesus, The Christ, as my Lord and Savior. Now, as a teenage mother, I attempted genuine romantic relationships again, still without knowing premarital sex was fornication. Two years later, I began to *transform* by the Word of God. I learned about fornication and practiced abstinence by choice for the first time. It wasn't a *perfect* walk; I still had moments of weakness. From the time I was first raped to learning about fornication, did I have anger and pain under the sweet personality? Yes. Yet, I had no shame. It was supernatural.

Knowing who I am in Christ and the mere fact that there is NEVER a reason for *shame* IF you simply **don't** give other people's opinions *power* to dictate to your identity—results in NO shame. **I have NO shame.** I've never experienced *shame* or guilt—not due to *my* power but God's Power within. Other's opinions never mattered my whole life. A few years later, after accepting Jesus, I discovered God had given me the **ministry of deliverance** and, specifically, deliverance from *shame*.

So know this: Other people's opinions and our enemy Satan's words about you should NEVER trump God's opinion of you…EVER! Now, you may be asking yourself…

"So what IS God's opinion of me?"

Here is the **answer**, to list a few, from the HEART **of God**—His WORD—**about** YOU (*Bold words are highlighted by the author for emphasis.*):

1. "I praise you because **I am fearfully and wonderfully made; your works are wonderful**, I know that full well." *(Psalm 139:14, NIV)*

2. "But you are a **chosen people**, a **royal priesthood**, a **holy nation**, **God's special possession**, that you may declare the praises of him who called you out of darkness into his wonderful light." *(1 Peter 2:9, NIV)*

3. "For we are **God's handiwork**, created in Christ Jesus to do good works, which God prepared in advance for us to do." *(Ephesians 2:10, NIV)*

4. "Are not two sparrows sold for a penny? Yet not one of them will fall to the ground outside your Father's care. And even the very hairs of your head are all numbered. So don't be afraid; **you are worth more than many sparrows**." *(Matthew 10:29–31, NIV)*

5. "…for in Christ Jesus you are all **sons of God**, through faith." *(Galatians 3:26, ESV)*

6. "Therefore, if anyone is in Christ, he is a **new creation**. The old has passed away; behold, the new has come." *(2 Corinthians 5:17, ESV)*

7. "…and to put on the new self, **created after the likeness of God in true righteousness and holiness**." *(Ephesians 4:24, ESV)*

8. "You are the **salt of the earth**, but if salt has lost its taste, how shall its saltiness be restored? It is no longer good for anything except to be thrown out and trampled under people's feet." *(Matthew 5:13, ESV)*

9. "…he predestined us for adoption to himself as **sons through Jesus Christ**, according to the purpose of his will…." (*Ephesians 1:5, ESV*)

10. "If we confess our sins, he is faithful and just to **forgive us** *our* sins and to **cleanse us** from all unrighteousness." (*1 John 1:9, KJV*)

11. "You are the **light of the world**. A city set on a hill cannot be hidden." (*Matthew 5:14, NKJV*)

12. "…but **God shows his love for us** in that while we were still sinners, **Christ died for us**." (*Romans 5:8, ESV*)

13. "No longer do I call you servants, for the servant does not know what his master is doing; but I have called you **friends**, for all that I have heard from my Father I have made known to you." (*John 15:15, ESV*)

14. "Go therefore and **make disciples of all nations**, baptizing them in the name of the Father and of the Son and of the Holy Spirit…." (*Matthew 28:19, NKJV*)

15. "But **you will receive power** when the Holy Spirit has come upon you, and **you will be my witnesses** in Jerusalem and in all Judea and Samaria, and to the end of the earth." (*Acts 1:8, ESV*)

16. "Or do you not know that **your body is a temple of the Holy Spirit within you**, whom you have from God? **You are not your own**…." (*1 Corinthians 6:19, ESV*)

It is what it is…so SMILE!

Also know, THIS is partially why you are so hated by Lucifer (God's angel turned our enemy). You are extremely valuable, loved, precious, and SPECIAL to God.

Now moving on…

The second you make a new ***present*** decision, the prior *choices* become *past* decisions. You are NOT a *prisoner* of them, whether they were *right*, *wrong*, or *indifferent*. They are, in fact, EXTREMELY **powerful** because they reflect the **nature of God** within your *present* state.

God's Nature towards you is not a fairy tale, full of fluff and merely words. His nature reflects **love**, **power**, **mercy**, **grace**, **deliverance**, **passion** for us, and **promises** ("…to keep you…" [Jude 1:24], "plans to prosper you" and "give you an expected end" [Jeremiah 29:11]), to name a few.

Your *past* decisions are *extremely* valuable and make up your life story and testimony full of God's Love and Wisdom. Share it unapologetically!

Without *past* decisions, good or bad, resulting in **victories** and **wounds**, "we could not be a part of the Body of Christ which was also 'wounded'…" as one of my former teachers would so eloquently state. VALUE *past* decisions for what they are and the purpose they serve. Learn from them and GROW!

Again, what's GREAT about all five types of decisions is that NONE are made in vain. God will use them ALL to benefit us (if we love Him) and to win in LIFE!

God's Continuous "Unacknowledged" Giving

Our decisions do not stop God's Giving. The Bible is full of scriptures that show how God **gives** us many things as well as "removes" many things. We make decisions daily—*right*, *wrong*, good, and bad—yet God never stops giving "things" to us (for example, from air to breathe to unseen favor with man).

God *gives* us *more* things that mankind is UNAWARE of (regarding what is actually *given by Him*) than aware of. People typically reduce the gifts from God to man's abilities (gifts, talents, intelligence, etc.) and works (accomplishments, good deeds, etc.), and they *take the credit* for the results. They commonly refer to the results as *"blessings"* yet subconsciously believe the results are "due" to their actions. In fact, it is quite the opposite.

God does honor our actions that reflect Him, and the ability to do so is through gifts from Him. But understand, the **results** from the gifts *God gives us (our abilities and works)* have **nothing** to do with us nor our "goodness" in the greater spectrum of things. No abilities, works, or actions can **earn** anything from God. **Everything He gives us is a gift**, *including* the results of our obedience.

Will God require a "prerequisite" (a willing *choice* of obedience on *our part*) to initiate a *move of God*? Yes. But ultimately, when God moves on our behalf for His Glory and we experience the results, these are ALSO His gifts *given* to us that we do not deserve. He is constantly and consistently *giving* to us!

This means God does not stop *giving* because of our *wrong* decisions! In fact, He continuously *gives* us so much—regardless of *any* of our decisions—most of it is *unacknowledged*.

In Conclusion...

ALL decisions have **VALUE**. The underlying common denominator for all decisions is…they are ALL valuable. Regarding *right, wrong, past, present,* and *future* decisions, their **ultimate** value is revealed in time. In regard to *present* and *future* decisions, they are ***ideally*** made through patience and knowing what God wants you to do.

Understanding the value of decisions helps you to understand the importance of *choices* and *options*. *Options create choices…and choices create the details of decisions*.

Acknowledging *and* understanding the attributes of decisions—specifically past, present, and future decisions—will help you to make wise *choices* in life, including those pertaining to **marriage**.

Regardless of *past* mistakes made in major areas of life (romantic relationships, careers, home regions, family, etc.), as long as we have life and learn from them, we have the power, *option*, and *choice* to make *new* decisions that lead us to *destined choices and desires*.

New knowledge, understanding, and revelation aid this process. Reading this book is a major start.

Some of our powerful testimonies are ready to be shared, and some are still in the making. Every decision you've ever made and will make has a part to play in your amazing, unique story that reveals the Glory of God…in your powerful testimony…as part of your life's story… shared by you and observed by others!

CHAPTER Fifteen

"SIMPLE" TRUTHS ABOUT CHOICES & OPTIONS

Over the years, while under the sound pastoral teachings of Apostles Dr. Fred L. Hodge, Jr. and Mrs. Linda Hodge, I had heard repetitious, highly effective lessons regarding decision-making, including but not limited to the following statement:

"Never make a permanent decision off a temporary situation."

I'd like to further add *another* way to examine this powerful statement as it relates to the correlation between *choices* and *options*....

"Never make permanent <u>choices</u> based on temporary <u>options</u>."
- Krista Nicole

How you **view** various *options* and what you **consider** *options* will change as *you* change.

As the fascination of this topic, "Choices," increased throughout the years and produced more and more understanding, more *"simple truths about **choices** and **options**"* were revealed. Yet the premise of them ALL are the following scriptures:

> **DEUTERONOMY 30:19, ESV**
>
> I call heaven and earth to witness against you today, that I have set before you
> life and death, blessing and curse. Therefore **choose** life,
> that you and your offspring may live,

> **DEUTERONOMY 30:15-16, NIV**
>
> ¹⁵ See, I set before you today life and prosperity, death and destruction.
>
> ¹⁶ For I **command** you today to love the Lord your God, to walk in obedience to him, and to keep his commands, decrees and laws; then you **will** live and increase, and the Lord your God will bless you in the land you are entering to **possess**.

God set before us these *options* because He desires to be loved, obeyed, honored, and *chosen* by our own free will. As a result, He gives us true life, full of increase, and a blessed state as we enter into His promises.

Your *choices* in life are up to you! God **loves** you so much, He has given you the ***principle*** instruction that governs **ALL**!

(Some of the *"'Simple' Truths"* refer to the definitions of *"Wants," "Needs,"* and *"Desires"* [various types of people] derived from this book.)

The "Milk"

1. It is our free will that creates *options*, and our *choices* are the byproduct.

2. Don't let things you *want* that really don't matter (in the larger scope of things) stop you from *choosing* and receiving God's best for you!

3. Attraction to those who are *"Wants"* (and your perceived *wants*) generally derive from short-term preferences that naturally change over time. So why base a permanent, long-term decision on a temporary *situation*, a temporary *choice,* a temporary *want,* or a temporary *personal desire*?

4. Those who are *"Wants"* (or your perceived *wants*) are commonly mistaken as those who are *"Needs"* (or your perceived *needs*). When you know the types by definition, you can distinguish the difference to know when God is guiding you or you are guiding yourself.

5. We tend to *not* give God the opportunity to give us our *needs* (or those who are *"Needs"*) because our *wants* (or those who are *"Wants"*) are in the way.

6. God will only grant you what He knows you will give HIM glory for. Understand, obedience *is* better than sacrifice because sacrifice benefits you; obedience benefits you and others. Accepting what God grants benefits you and others and is a form of obedience. Obedience is an act of love for the Father God. Accept what God grants, and glorify HIM.

7. Because men are designed to innately "find" a wife and ways to provide and protect, they regularly practice the process of elimination. Over time, they know what they *do* and *don't* want—and need and don't need. This skill is a must and "sharpened" over time. This skill aids in discerning the *destined choice*.

8. Supernaturally, there is a *draw* towards a certain person, place, thing, or idea, created by an *innate desire* from your heart and spirit. It is referred to as a "knowing." The *option* (or *"Option"*/person) that has this *draw* is the *Godly desire* (or *"Desire"*/person).

9. Our *desires* are our *personal wants*. God's *desires* are our true *needs* and *wants* (also known as a *"Needed Want"*/person).

10. Once you identify an interest, do not make a permanent decision based on one's "trial period" *Representative*. The "Representative" is the first personality layer: the surface person you meet and the side of the person that is aimed to "impress" you. The *trial period* is typically during the first one to two years. But God *is* moving *faster*! Therefore, in this dispensation, the *trial period* is generally one to six months; this is a general guide/"rule of thumb" for understanding God's ways and the times we are living in. FOLLOW the Holy Spirit, who knows the perfect and exact timing to move forward with decisions.

11. Don't mistake physical "attraction" for a *need*. It is a *want*, and God knows what we *want*. We *want* to enjoy who we look at every day. He will *give* you a *desire* for a person you will enjoy looking at daily.

12. Just because you think someone is attractive does not mean you have to or should be with them. You can enjoy one's attractiveness from afar.

The "Meat"

13. *Choices* are the street corners on a map. Every turn leads us closer to our destiny or further away from our destiny and God's Will.

14. When *choices* are made that seem to lead you away from God's Plans, you will always find your way back to destiny if you love and obey the Lord.

15. *Decisions* shape and create our life story.

16. When God brings two people ("*Needs*") together who accept becoming each other's "desire," one *Desire* cannot turn off the other *Desire*. The person God chose has always been and will remain *more* than *good enough* and the BEST *choice*.

17. Not knowing what *choice* to make is a great thing! "New things start in the dark... Faith life is blind life... ['Lean not to your own understanding...' Proverbs 3:5]." *(Apostle Dr. Matthew Stevenson, III)*

18. In between *desiring* the Will of God and *knowing* the Will of God, you will experience intimacy with God.

19. In between *knowing* the Will of God and *experiencing* the Will of God, you will learn to trust God. (inspired by former pastor)

20. Whatever you keep your mind on, your affections will follow. You must manage your thoughts, imagination, heart, ears, and mouth.

21. "God's Will is not automatically revealed. You have to ask [God] for it." (former teacher)

22. "Anything that is *not* what you are believing God for [specifically mates], do not entertain it." (former teacher)

23. "Everything you want [and need] to do will come from *your desire*. God *gives* us the *desire* to do ['for it is God who works in you to both will and to do for *His* good pleasure.' Philippians 2:13]. He won't *give* a *desire* contrary to His Will." (former teacher)

24. BEFORE making a decision, ask yourself, *"Am I seeking God's Will?"* (also known as God's Plan)

25. When your heart *desires* God's Will, He *gives* it to you.

26. The manifestation of God's Plan starts with *your desire* to *choose* it. *Choices* required to live out HIS plan become clearer, and the decision becomes easier to make.

27. "If there is something you *desire* outside of the Holy Spirit, there is potential for deception." (former teacher)

28. Your life is the sum total of both obedient and disobedient *choices* made in the past.

29. When you know who you are, you don't chase *options* (or "*Options*"/people). (Pray these words daily…"*I thank you, Lord Jesus, The Christ, that it is rhema that I know who I am in Christ*"—until you know who you are and BELIEVE it.)

30. "If you are not sure why you want 'it' now, then more than likely, you will have a problem handling all that 'it' brings. Wait, reassess, then revisit your *desire* for 'it.' Even if your *desire* does not change, you will still be the wiser in preparing for 'it.'" (former teacher)

31. "God's *choice* [*desire*] for you [regarding a marriage mate or partner] will share your same core values." (former pastor)

32. The way you view *options* (or "*Options*"/people) determines how you *choose*.

33. "God is not backing up anything He did not do." (former teacher)

34. "Your *choices* create your possibilities." (former pastor)

So let's end with this…

1 JOHN 2:3-6, NIV

We know that we have come to know him if we keep his commands.

⁴ Whoever says, 'I know him,' but does not do what he commands is a liar, and the truth is not in that person.

⁵ But if anyone obeys his word, love for God is truly made complete in them. This is how we know we are in him:

⁶ Whoever claims to live in him must live as Jesus did.

1 JOHN 2:15-17, NIV

Do not love the world or anything in the world. If anyone loves the world, love for the Father is not in them.

¹⁶ For everything in the world—the lust of the flesh, the lust of the eyes, and the pride of life—comes not from the Father but from the world.

¹⁷ The world and its desires pass away, but whoever does the will of God lives forever.

My Final Words to You…

Living in the Will of God is worth every second invested to *learn* and know *what* His Will is for you that has been preordained and **planned** (Ephesians 1:5, 1:11; Romans 8:29–30)! It starts with renewing your mind!

So congratulations! By reading this book, enriched with God's Word, you have been "transformed by the renewing of your mind." As you "do the Word of God, you WILL discern what is the good, acceptable, and perfect Will of God" (Romans 12:2) for marriage!

Knowing *who's who* and *what's what* and God's Timing are MAJOR parts of what you will discern, and this understanding will *reveal* His Will—God's divine plans for YOUR Kingdom marriage on Earth as you *desire* to know!

"Do not be anxious about your life" (Matthew 6:25, ESV). "For your heavenly Father knows that you **need** all these things. But seek **first** the kingdom of God and His righteousness, and **all** these things shall be added to you" (Matthew 6:32–33, NKJV). As you seek God, your relationship with Him will build and revelation will be revealed regarding marriage. "Blessed are those who hunger and thirst for righteousness, For they shall be **filled**" (Matthew 5:6, NKJV).

The marriage God preordained with the person He *chose* will enhance your life with God, intimacy with God, and your walk with God. It's bigger than marriage.

So again, I say congratulations! You are well on your way to enjoying the powerful and rewarding marriage God intended for YOU! So smile!

You have delighted yourself in the LORD and He will "give you the *desires* of your heart" (Psalm 37:4). You are **equipped with understanding** on how to "seek first the Kingdom of God and His righteousness" and for *destined choices* based on the Word of God…and for *God's divine plans for marriage*!

❝

MATTHEW 6:33, ESV
But seek first the kingdom of God and his righteousness,
and all these things will be added to you.

Thank you for reading this book!

Your support really means a lot to me!

Please write a **review**! I would love to hear your feedback and how this book has benefited you!

Your review will also help other readers know what to expect and encourage them to read it as well!

I really appreciate it!

-Krista Nicole

GodsDivinePlansForMarriage.com

ABOUT THE AUTHOR

Krista Nicole is a devout woman of God, mother, author, actress, musician, inspirational speaker, and a behavioral specialist for over fifteen years. She has experienced and survived a tumultuous marriage that gained her wisdom, knowledge, and insight to assist others in understanding the importance of personal development (spiritually, emotionally, and mentally) and choice-making prior to marriage and after divorce.

She earned a Bachelor of Arts in Social Sciences at California State University, Northridge, majoring in political science with an emphasis on government and pre-law. She has a strong passion for sociology and the study of human behavior. She also has an equally strong passion for human justice and practical, Godly wisdom to guide and apply for the betterment of people's lives. She understands life is full of choices, and wisdom assists humanity in making the best choices possible for the one life we are all given as a gift from God. She believes, "the better our choices are, the better our life experience will be."

As a teacher and Christian minister, she has written a guide to understand *who* is *who* and *what* is *what* as it pertains to potential mates by gaining a newfound perspective on how to view *options* to make destiny-driven *choices*.

Her love for all people of the world—irrespective of their religious beliefs, cultural differences, and life experiences—has birthed compassion to help others improve their personal character to become their best selves in order to make the best choices in life. She has a passion for others to experience God's plans, His perfect Will for their lives, and the Kingdom Marriage they both deserve and *desire*.

www.ingramcontent.com/pod-product-compliance
Lightning Source LLC
Chambersburg PA
CBHW060947050426
42337CB00052B/1624